Dearest Sunn

"Merry Christma:

Hope you en[j]d
read.

Love always
Nan e Grandad.
xxxxxx

CW00631319

2012/.

HOW TO PLAY CRICKET

HOW TO PLAY CRICKET

SIR DONALD BRADMAN

HOW TO PLAY CRICKET

INTRODUCTION

WHEN I was a very small boy, cricket was to me the most wonderful game in the world (and, of course, it still is). Unfortunately, however, being some distance from the metropolis, I was unable to witness any first-class cricketers in action. Actually, with the exception of a small portion of one Test Match, I saw no first-class cricket whatever until I was engaged in playing for New South Wales myself. Neither did I have the opportunity of reading any books on cricket by world-famous players. Consequently, my entire cricketing experience has been a practical one.

In this book I have made every endeavor to put as clearly and concisely as possible all the ideas gained over a period of years.

So far as batting is concerned, I feel that my record in Test Matches is the best justification of my methods. By means of the written word, I trust I may be able to assist some of the cricketers of today, but mainly the cricketers of the future.

I do hope the value of my experience will be within the reach of everybody who cares to read this little volume. In these pages I have advocated what I conscientiously believe to be the best and most effective method of playing the grand old game.

Please do not think, however, that what I have written

must be copied by all and sundry; every cricketer living has his own individuality, and must be allowed to express it. These methods, however, are mine, and as far as possible I play 100 per cent along the lines set out in this volume. Naturally, existing conditions do at all times dictate the type of cricket to be played.

Herein you will find no difficult scientific explanations. I have purposely avoided them. Practical common sense in one's play is very often more effective than any textbook can be.

So, then, may I ask you to read slowly and at your leisure? Imagine I am chatting to you, not in the role of a dictator, but in the role of a friend, saying quietly, "Playing in this manner has given me the best results. Have you tried that way? If not, it may assist you. Let us talk it over. Perhaps between us your game can be improved."

And, after all, is not that the spirit of cricket?

Don Bradman

CONTENTS

ILLUSTRATIONS (facing pages)

HOW TO PLAY CRICKET

THE BEGINNINGS

WHEN writing a book it occurs to me that the most practical way of going about it is to do what a cricketer has to do, that is, start from the bottom of the ladder and work up.

A boy cannot become a Test Match player until he has been through the usual preliminary stages, perhaps to the extent of playing in the back-yard with a kerosene tin for a wicket, perhaps a portion of a tree for a bat, and so on. Neither can a boy become a brilliant stroke player overnight in any class of cricket.

Consequently, I propose to deal with the various stages gradually, setting out each little factor in turn, and right now I would like to stress these factors which, no matter how insignificant they may appear on paper, are to my mind just as important in their respective places as those other items which are generally regarded as more important.

Take first of all the lad of a few summers. Maybe he has just started school. Maybe he is not yet old enough, but he wants to play with something. The natural desire in the majority of cases is to pick up a bat and ball. Armed with these two things, plus the company of the boy next door (or, if that boy's company is not available, perhaps his own will suffice), away he goes for a game.

Some mothers and fathers want to equip their boys with first-class equipment when they are still at a very tender age. If this can be done, well and good. If not, there is no harm done. Practically speaking, almost any old bat and any old ball will do in these early stages.

Those of my readers who are familiar with my cricketing career will recall how I started to play as a boy. My bat was not a piece of nice English willow, it was a very old small stump. My ball was not a genuine Wisden six-stitcher, it was an old golf ball found on the neighbouring golf links, where I had wandered in the hope of being able to carry somebody's golf clubs.

It is only reasonable for me to say I found hitting a small golf ball with a small stump much harder than hitting a cricket ball with a real cricket bat, and here is where the value of those early days came in. Playing with such a small ball and small bat must have trained my eyesight. This commenced for me a ground work.

Pardon the length to which I have gone in explaining what occurred in my youth, but I want to impress upon you the need for training a youngster in the art of hitting a ball. This is more important to a young boy (at least, I think so) than telling him how he must hold his left arm, and sundry other stereotyped matters.

But then the lad grows up. His hand increases in size. He goes to school and becomes a member of the school eleven. Now, of course, he has reached the stage of learning more about the art of cricket. No longer will any old bat or ball do. He must use a real cricket bat and cricket ball, even though it may be only a composition ball.

Just one more piece of advice, while the lad is still comparatively small. You cannot possibly expect a boy of ten years to wield a full-size cricket bat. To the father who is buying a lad a bat for his birthday, may I suggest you endeavour at all times to select him one which is well within his capacity to wield with a maximum amount of effect. I have experienced the desire of a boy to take hold of that beautiful full-sized piece of willow, knowing I could not use it properly, but ambitious just the same. It is wise for boys to curb this desire. Your turn will come, and very quickly, too.

When the opportunity arises for a little practice on the nearby wicket, it is also unwise for a boy to tax his strength in trying to bowl the ball 22 yards when he may just as easily pitch the wickets 15 yards apart, thereby conserving his energy, and helping him to be more accurate at a stage when it is imperative for him to learn the value of accuracy in bowling.

BATTING

SELECTING A BAT

NOW we pass along. Let us assume the lad has reached the stage of being able to use a real man's bat. His desire to go into a big city sports store, where there are hundreds of beautiful blades ready for inspection, is about to be fulfilled. Probably he has glanced at them before with longing eyes, not daring to touch. What are the main essentials in selecting a bat for one's own private use?

Here is where I have always adopted a single-minded course, which has undoubtedly proved a successful one.

Try and realise this fact. No matter how beautiful the willow may be, it cannot possibly be of any value unless you can hit the ball when and where you like.

The manufacturers of cricket bats know considerably more about the quality of willow than probably 99 per cent of cricketers; consequently I have always made the quality of the willow my last consideration.

Balance is the all-important essential. One may pick up a dozen bats in succession. Of these, eleven may feel just very nice. Immediately the twelfth one is handled, one exclaims: "What a beauty!" Why? Simply because it feels different; it appeals to you. And there you have the secret of selecting a bat. Nobody else can pick a bat for you. Pick one entirely on the way it feels in your hands. By doing this you will always have implicit faith in your bat.

When making a stroke, should you not hit the ball in the centre of the blade, you will not lay the blame on your bat. You know it suits you. It is not too heavy and not too light, therefore the reason you failed to make perfect connection with that ball was due to some human failing.

Throughout my experience of play in first-class cricket I have never once gone out to bat unless perfectly satisfied that my bat had the best balance of any I could possibly obtain, and I am certain it played no small part in my success in Test cricket.

PREPARING THE BLADE

IN the matter of preparing a bat before use there are various methods, any of which may prove quite satisfactory.

My own method has been to rub a thin coating of raw linseed oil on the face and edges of the blade, from the bottom of the splice to the bottom of the blade, once each day, about six times at least, before the first time of using.

If possible, it is always wise to use your bat carefully at first (against an old ball for preference) and without attempting to hit with too much force. In this manner the face is gradually prepared for harder usage. Later, when actually used in match play, I invariably rub a light coating of oil on the face of the blade after each game, before putting it away.

Another most important feature is to have the rubber on the bat handle glued down tightly. On numerous occasions

I have seen players lose their wicket through failure to guard against this very simple but common fault.

PADS AND BATTING GLOVES

I CAN still remember, and it is not so very long ago, boys being called "sissies" because they dared to wear batting gloves. Pads were admitted, but batting gloves were looked upon with disdain.

I think that day is now passed. The question of being brave or being afraid no longer arises.

Cricket is a game and, for the majority who participate therein, a pastime which is solely indulged in for Saturday afternoon's pleasure. No one wants to have his fingers damaged or his hand injured when it can be avoided, but in playing cricket a smack on the fingers from a ball which rises suddenly often occurs quite accidentally. Therefore it behoves every young cricketer always to wear batting gloves and leg guards. Naturally, the better quality they are the better the protection afforded the player.

There are various types of batting gloves, but mainly we may classify them into two sections—those with the open palm and the ones of the gauntlet type where the whole hand is closed.

Players must make their choice according to their individual tastes. Both are illustrated at page 16. Personally, I prefer the open palm. It seems to allow more freedom, and gives one a better feel of the bat handle.

I am aware how uncomfortable batting gloves may feel

GLOVE

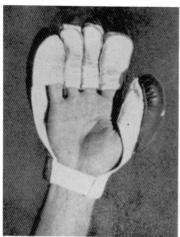

This type of open palm batting glove allows a better "feel" of the bat handle, and is my own personal choice (see page 16.)

GLOVE

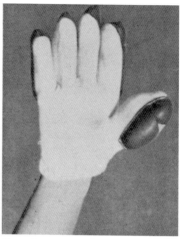

Gauntlet type of batting glove. Very popular with players whose hands are inclined to perspire. The cotton absorbs the perspiration, and prevents one's hands slipping on the rubber (see page 16.)

BATTING GRIP

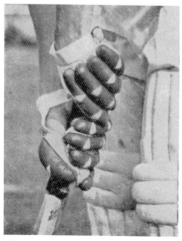

The batting grip, showing the hands close together for an easy swing (see page 19.)

BOOT

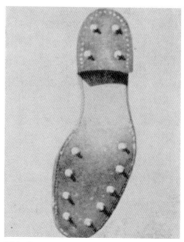

This is an exact replica of the sole of one of my boots. The position and number of the sprigs have proved ideal under all conditions (see page 17.)

Showing toe *on* popping-crease line. This position is not correct, and a batsman could be stumped when his toe was on the line. He would not be *within* his crease.

Correct position of toe — just behind or within the popping crease, but allowing no margin for "drag".

The position I advocate in my description, with the toe well behind the popping crease as above; not only is the batsman within his ground, but he also has a margin in which to move in case of over-balancing or dragging the foot.

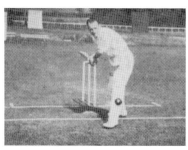

FORWARD DEFENCE (see page 23)

BACK DEFENCE (see page 24)

OFF DRIVE (see page 26)

at first. After a few innings, however, this will disappear, and in its stead will come greater confidence.

Whilst on the subject of leg guards, it is always wise to see that each buckle is properly adjusted, with none of those unsightly loose strap ends hanging down. If they are your own pads, adjust them properly and then cut off the overhanging parts which are not required. Otherwise, a similar but less satisfactory effect may be gained by tucking the straps in behind the leg guard.

FOOTWEAR

ONLY after playing in a hot Australian sun in Test Matches lasting up to eight days, on the hardest cricket grounds, can one fully appreciate the value of and the need for comfortable, properly designed footwear.

Naturally, each player should select his own pair of boots, and see they fit him properly.

When it comes to fitting the sprigs in them, it is remarkable the number of persons one meets who plaster the soles of their boots with all kinds of sprigs, in all manner of positions.

It is not necessary to put many sprigs in a boot, but what one does use should be in the correct places—firm, and reasonably sharp. Sprigs can usually be obtained which will prove quite suitable when driven in with a hammer, but I have found a better method.

If one gets running spikes built into the soles of the boot by a bootmaker they cannot come out; they cannot get loose, they will retain a reasonably sharp point and last for years. Every pair of boots I own is sprigged in this manner, and the sprigs are placed in the positions as shown in the photographs at page 16. Once this has been done, the sprigs will probably require no further attention, otherwise, the player is continually using the hammer and boot-last (probably with disastrous effects to his thumb).

And do not forget to keep those boots clean.

Here is another valuable tip. By wearing heavy knitted socks (or two pairs of ordinary socks) your feet will stand the strain much better. A single pair of thin socks scarcely provides sufficient protection.

Another hint which may prove of value is this. When playing on an uneven surface, or when the ground is wet and slippery, the simple precaution of securely binding the ankles before taking the field may prevent a serious injury.

Failure to do this on one occasion caused me to spend three weeks in hospital, and a further two months' convalescence. There is no reason why you should have the same experience.

Incidentally, that reminds me of another experience I once had—reading the report of my own death in a newspaper. Rather an unusual occurrence. However, I am straying from the point.

Surely it is unnecessary for me at this juncture once again to impress upon players the need for keeping all their cricketing attire in the best possible condition.

Nice white pads and boots, coupled with clean and well-pressed clothes, are essential if one is to remember that old,

old saying: "If you cannot be a cricketer you can at least look like one."

THE GRIP

WE have now reached the subject upon which the leading players of the world have different ideas, both in theory and in practice.

Give a boy a cricket bat, or any piece of timber equivalent to a cricket bat, and ask him to swing it horizontally as hard as he possibly can at a given object. What will be the result? Simply this. The boy will grip that bat in his most natural manner in an endeavour to get the maximum amount of power into the blow. There he has immediately the basis of what would be his natural grip of a cricket bat. I use the word "his" advisedly, because the natural grip of one boy may vary slightly from that of another.

At all times I am a great believer in building up the natural ideas or peculiar gifts of each individual.

Generally, you will find that the hands will be close together. A small portion of the handle will protrude above the left hand (in the case of a right-hander), whilst a larger portion still will be clearly shown between the bottom of the right hand and the top of the blade of the bat. Just grip a bat in this fashion. Swing it like a pendulum backwards and forwards. You will find how much easier it is to swing with the hands close together than it is when one hand is held at the top of the handle and the other at the bottom. In this latter case we find the hands working in opposition to each other instead of in harmony.

The position of the right hand is easily defined in this manner. Hold a bat in front of you in the right hand only, face downward, the V between the thumb and first finger of the right hand will be clearly visible. This V should be strictly in a line with the centre of the back of the bat. Continue holding the bat in this manner in the right hand only, and allowing your right arm to hang in the most natural position at your side—if your right-hand grip is correct you will find that the face of the bat will be at right angles to your foot, and pointing behind you.

Now the left hand. Here is where the experts differ.

There are two methods: one favoured by one school, one favoured by another. Both must be correct, results having proved that, but each individual player must decide for himself which of the two grips suits his particular style of play. The best way I can illustrate these two grips is as follows:

Take a bat and grip it in your natural way, and play an ordinary defensive stroke with a perfectly straight bat. Either your left wrist will be in front of the bat handle facing toward the bowler, or it will be behind the bat handle almost facing towards your chest. The former method is probably more universally used than the latter, but whichever style suits you personally, then do not alter that particular style for any other, which evidently is not your natural grip.

For myself, I favour keeping the left wrist behind the handle for all ordinary strokes, with one exception.

I can use either grip with equal comfort and results,

but in making a pull shot my natural grip has given me an advantage which I would otherwise lose, and which I will explain at a later stage when dealing with that shot.

When making such strokes as the ordinary straight drive, the hands will not change their position on the handle, but when playing a back defensive stroke (and perhaps one or two other strokes, such as the leg glance), better control of the bat is often obtained by allowing the right hand to slip down to the bottom of the handle. When this is done, a loss of attacking power naturally follows. For the purposes I have just mentioned, however, no attacking power is required, but rather accuracy and control. The illustrations at page 16 should help to clarify my remarks as to the positions of the hands.

STANCE

ONCE more we touch upon a subject where leading cricketers adopt slightly different methods, but on this occasion I really believe a principle can be set which should be followed by every player.

When considering your stance, remember these essentials. You must be comfortable. You must be well balanced. You must be able to play either forward or back with equal speed. You must be able to watch the bowler easily with both eyes, and without strain. If you can do these things, your stance cannot be far wrong.

To be comfortable is more or less a matter of taking up your stance in a natural, easy position. The best way to be perfectly balanced, I find, is to have the weight equally distributed on both feet, these being approximately nine inches to one foot apart.

The bat may rest upon the ground either in front of or behind the right toe, according to your own desires, but make sure the handle is not in such a position that it may catch in your pads or clothes when you are about to make a stroke.

Both feet, as a general rule, should run parallel to the popping crease. If they are not, you will probably find one foot is carrying more weight than the other, thereby upsetting your balance. The inside edge of the back foot should be at least three inches behind the popping crease in order to allow yourself a slight margin for dragging the toe when playing forward. Remember, the inside edge of the popping crease (i.e., the edge nearest the stumps) is the line you must be behind, not the outer edge.

BLOCK

WHEN taking up his position at the wicket, every player must take block, the reason being to provide himself with a guide as to the position of his feet and his body relative to the stumps.

It is immaterial what block is taken, so long as the player remembers the position he did take, and plays accordingly.

I have always found the leg stump the most serviceable block of all, because in taking up that position I am always certain that a ball delivered in a line with my legs must be outside the leg stump, whilst anything within range of the off-stump or directed at the bat, I know to be tolerably close to straight. This, of course, gives me the clue for stroke making, and automatically guides my mind in deciding what stroke to make from each delivery. However, should you be in the habit of taking centre, or centre and leg, for your block, then do not let my experience make you change unless you are satisfied such a change would help your batsmanship.

DEFENSIVE PLAY

HAVING assimilated the vital points up to this stage, the player now prepares to go to the wicket.

Of course every cricketer realises how much experience may be gained at the practice nets. Here is the place to develop your play.

All manner of experiments may be carried out at your discretion, in order to determine the methods upon which you are to model your future career.

The first arts every batsman must master are forward defensive play and back defensive play. If you can play every scoring stroke in cricket to perfection, they will avail you nothing unless you have a sound defence to guide you when facing a ball from which you cannot make a scoring shot. And the higher the class of cricket in which you play, the more pronounced will become the necessity for this defence.

There is no rule as to which particular kind of ball demands a certain type of defensive stroke, but in my own play I have adopted a principle which I endeavour to follow, and which has helped me considerably. It is this: When a ball is pitched so far up that I can, by playing forward, smother any break which may be on the ball, then I play forward. Unless I can be certain of smothering the break, I always play back. Being rather short of stature means my reach when playing forward is very limited, consequently I am forced to play back more than the average player. A very tall individual would probably play forward much more than he would play back, because of his physical advantages in this respect.

When playing forward make sure that you always play with a perfectly straight bat, and endeavour to allow the ball to meet the bat just before the latter reaches the absolute perpendicular. Should the bat reach the perpendicular before making contact with the ball there will be a tendency to hit the ball up in the air, and a catch may result.

The only movement of the feet when playing forward is that of the left foot, which goes towards the line of flight of the ball in a natural manner.

When playing back the same principles apply, in that the bat should be kept straight and should make contact with the ball just before reaching the perpendicular. This time, however, more movement of the feet is necessary. Move the right foot back and across in front of the wicket— bring the left foot across until the pads are practically touching, and then play the ball with your bat in front of your pads. The pads should be directly between where the ball pitches and the stumps.

If the bat is held loosely in the hands when playing back, we get the effect of what is known as a dead bat. The ball on striking a bat held loosely will find no impelling force to direct it on its way, and will therefore fall almost straight down on to the ground. The use of this dead bat may be very valuable on a difficult wicket, when infieldsmen are placed close to the bat waiting for a catch.

In describing this method of playing back I have given you my own idea of doing so. In that fashion I find it easier to see the ball and to watch its flight.

By playing forward or back along the lines indicated here, one is generally ready to take advantage of the slightest inaccuracy of length on the part of the bowler. The ball slightly overpitched may be driven, if you are ready to drive it, and of course you should be ready.

The ball slightly underpitched may be pulled or dealt with by some other effective stroke.

Here, then, we have the basis or the foundation of batsmanship. Defence. That should be your watchword, and every cricketer should regard his defence as the builder does the foundation of his house.

I always advocate using the bat as the first line of defence, only utilising the pads as a second line of defence when the bat has been beaten.

Whilst the present l.b.w. rule exists, a batsman is more or less forced to cover the stumps with his legs when playing a back defensive stroke to a spin bowler. If he doesn't he will give the bowler a considerable advantage. By covering the wicket with the legs correctly, a batsman could not be bowled by any ball, thereby defeating the objects of a spin bowler.

With the l.b.w. rule which operated in the 1920s and early 1930s, it was reasonably safe to pad-up against any turning ball. Batsmen veered towards a slightly different technique, however, when the off-side l.b.w. was introduced.

Under the new rule it is regarded as much safer to play forward to an off-break. Then, if the ball turns enough to beat the bat, the break is usually sufficient to negative an l.b.w. appeal.

By playing back, the batsman gives the bowler a better opportunity of trapping him l.b.w. with the pads close to the stumps.

Regrettably, this new rule tends to cause a preponderance of ungainly forward lunges, coupled with the presence of one or two short-leg fieldsmen.

It rather stifles the batsman's urge for a full-blooded pull-shot off the back foot, making him play safe. Yet the vicious pull will, more than any other shot, destroy the effectiveness of the bowler, or even remove those menacing close-in fielders. I prefer to see a batsman trust his eye and his confidence with the ball that is short of a length rather than his being negative.

To me, cricket approaches nearest to perfection when a great leg-spinner is bowling to a champion batsman. I like to think in terms of aggression—of bat versus ball and no other impedimenta.

But, so long as an l.b.w. law exists, coaches cannot be blamed for advising batsmen to use its protection. Style without success brings few rewards.

THE DRIVES

THERE are four very simple strokes in cricket, known as the on drive, straight drive, off drive, and cover drive.

In each case the stroke is made in practically the same manner, the chief difference lying in the direction in which the ball is hit. A short reference to my diagram at page 64 will immediately indicate the exact area these shots cover.

I need scarcely explain the centre of that portion of the field to which an on drive is made would be mid-on. Cover-point represents the centre of the area in which a cover drive would be made; similarly mid-off represents an off drive, whilst a straight drive would pass close to the wicket at the bowler's end.

These four drives are primarily forward strokes, the action of playing a forward defensive stroke really being the action of a straight drive, but in the former instance the object is a negative one, and the concluding movements appertaining to a drive have been checked.

In executing any of these drives one's original grip of the bat should be retained. A half volley is the ideal ball to drive, and whenever a drive is attempted all the power at the player's command should be put into the stroke.

A drive is a safe shot, practically the only danger arising when there is a tendency on the batsman's part to lift the ball. Every drive made should be intended for a positive scoring stroke. In the majority of cases, a boundary is aimed at, providing the placing of the ball is such as to defeat the fieldsmen's efforts to stop it.

To define just which drive to make must remain a matter for the judgment of the batsman. A perfectly straight half-volley on the middle stump would be an ideal ball to straight drive. A similar ball on the off stump would invite an off drive, on the leg stump an on drive, whilst three to six inches outside the off stump should mean work for the cover-point fieldsman. Whilst it is easy for me to indicate the ball to off drive as being one pitched on the off stump, such information would be valueless unless the batsman by his judgment can tell approximately where the ball is pitched. Consequently, in practice, one's strokes are largely governed by intuition.

The exact moment of impact when making a drive will be found to correspond with the forward defensive stroke. This will ensure keeping the ball on the ground.

With the exception of the cover drive, the full face of the bat always meets the ball when driving.

For a cover drive the blade must be angled very slightly towards the off, thereby cutting the ball in that direction. It may not be out of place to mention here that for this very reason a cover drive shows a tendency to veer towards point. Fieldsmen stationed at cover-point would do well to remember this fact.

Though I have seen few batsmen who could execute the strokes, every one of these four drives can also be played off the back foot to a short-pitched ball, so long as the ball does not rise too sharply from the pitch.

All the principles of a drive herein advocated may be followed in executing a drive off the back foot, in so far as they can apply.

By making a drive and playing forward, the left foot must be moved down the pitch and the weight transferred to the left foot as the stroke is being made. When driving off the back foot a short step towards the striker's wicket must be taken with the back foot, and the weight transferred to the back foot in executing the stroke. Here again we follow the outline of a back defensive stroke, but, as before, the action in making a drive is intensified, and the stroke carried through to a positive conclusion instead of a negative defensive position.

A perfectly straight bat must be employed. The bat should be brought down on the ball very hard. On account of the limited space at the batsman's disposal when driving off the back foot, tremendous wrist power is required, the forearms being used slightly, and the shoulders being almost eliminated. They merely assist in guiding the bat, and the power is obtained almost entirely from the wrists.

Any drive off the back foot is somewhat difficult, and as previously mentioned there are comparatively few batsmen who have mastered it, so do not be disappointed if your success in making these shots comes gradually. At the same time, perseverance to perfect these drives off the back foot, more particularly the one between the bowler and mid-on, will be amply rewarded. They are all potential match-winning shots.

SQUARE CUT

I AM told that the square cut was more popular a few years ago than it is today. No doubt this is brought about by the modern tendency on the part of the batsman to move always towards the line of flight of the ball instead of keeping the right foot anchored until the ball has been delivered. We generally see the batsman moving in front of the stumps as the bowler is running up.

The type of wicket and the type of bowling also have a large bearing on whether a batsman will attempt to square cut the ball.

The ball may be cut in the vicinity of point, but as a fieldsman is generally stationed at point, naturally the batsman desires to hit the ball slightly in front of, or slightly behind, point to get the ball past this man. In my efforts to do this, I have found it advantageous slightly to alter my method of making a cut in order to ensure greater accuracy in placing the ball.

When intending to hit the ball between point and cover point I move forward and across with the left foot, keeping the right foot in its original position. When I desire to place the ball just behind point I keep the left foot in its normal position and move across and slightly backwards with the right foot. A very short survey of the respective methods will quickly illustrate that, by using the latter, the ball is hit a fraction later, a fact which assists one to acquire greater accuracy.

The ideal ball to square cut would be considerably short of a good length and well outside the off stump. The more play one can give to the shoulders and forearms in combining with the wrists to make a square cut, the more power can be put into the blow.

The ball which rises approximately six inches above the level of the stumps would represent an ideal height for a ball to square cut. In saying this I am, of course, referring to a man of medium height. In all cases, readers must allow for some variation in all these strokes according to the stature of the batsman.

As when making a drive, I advocate hitting a square cut very hard. If, by a slight error of judgment, a ball is mishit, it will thus have a better chance of escaping the clutches of a fieldsman. With a perfectly hit ball a four will result instead of perhaps only a single. Once again the original grip of the bat remains unaltered in making the cut.

At the moment the ball is struck the bat will be as nearly horizontal as the height of the ball from the ground will allow. When the bat is not quite horizontal, the end of the blade will be slightly lower than the handle, and in order to send the ball towards the ground instead of up in the air the face of the bat must be turned slightly towards the ground as it makes contact with the ball. This point may be illustrated very clearly if you refer to the photograph at page 48 illustrating a cut.

DOWN THE GULLY

WITH a medium-pace or fast bowler operating to an off field, the single down the gully to third man fielding on the fence probably appears in the description of the play more than any other shot.

Actually it is only the square cut off the back foot, which I have just described, played a little later. To a good length ball, or preferably one short of a good length, outside the off stump, a stroke down the gully is very easy to make.

Go across and back with the right foot, getting well over towards the ball. Moving a little closer to it when making a cut down the gully is advisable, the back movement to be carried out in exactly the same manner, though a little less forcible in execution.

Unless there is a fieldsman close up in the gully this shot is reasonably safe, any danger lying in the possibility of a snick to the wicket-keeper or one of the slips. With a man in the gully the danger is increased considerably, and more care must be exercised, otherwise a catch may easily come his way. In fact, in recent times, I think I have seen more catches taken in the gully than in any other one position on the field excepting that of the wicket-keeper.

Considerable care must also be exercised in keeping the ball down when playing on a fiery wicket or one of two paces. The risk of mistiming a ball is obvious; therefore, it is wise to gauge carefully the factors which make for the safe execution of this shot before commencing to put it in operation.

BACK CUT

SOME critics may disagree with my naming of the shot through slips as the back cut. Sometimes I hear it referred to as the late cut, and there are one or two other names, but whatever you call it the ultimate intended destination of the ball is the same.

It is seldom in modern cricket that we see the back cut employed with any frequency, except, perhaps, by one or two true stylists. Once again I believe the habit of moving across in front of the stumps has materially helped to cut out this shot, which is probably as beautiful as any stroke in cricket.

My own grip when playing a back defensive shot. Notice the left wrist
behind the bat handle, which seems to give me greater control over the
bat (see page 23.)

Here we see a back defensive stroke with the left wrist in front of the back handle. This type of grip is more commonly used, yet does not suit me (see page 23.)

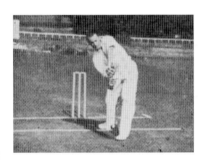 

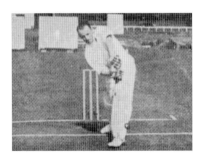 

COVER DRIVE (see page 26)

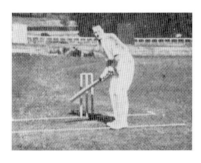 

STRAIGHT DRIVE (see page 27)

ON DRIVE (see page 28)

It can be employed when facing most types of bowlers, although the reward commensurate with the risk is greatest when opposing a medium-pace bowler. The extreme speed of a fast bowler makes the back cut at once a dangerous shot. Against the slow bowler we find the ball turning off the pitch, and even if the batsman makes the stroke correctly he will probably gain only one run if a fieldsman is stationed somewhere in the region of third man.

An immense amount of practice is required to perfect the shot. Such practice should of course be indulged in at the nets, for preference.

The all-important factor is to move the right foot well across towards the line of flight of the ball, so close in fact that the ball will probably pass little more than six inches outside the toe.

Unless the batsman moves across in this fashion, he may find himself hitting wildly at the ball instead of really caressing it as it passes by.

The back cut does not call for power, the stroke relies upon the speed which the bowler has imparted to the ball, but a slight flick of the wrists, and a tap from the bat as the ball passes by, will tend to increase that speed.

Moving across in the position previously indicated with the right foot, the bat may be brought down on to the ball in such a way that it is almost running parallel to the line of flight of the ball at the moment of contact. May I endeavour to make this a little more explicit. I have previously discussed the square cut wherein, at the moment of impact, you will find the bat is almost at right angles to the line of flight. With the back cut the position is directly the reverse.

One's bat just prior to contact with the ball will be almost parallel to the line of flight directly over the ball. Reference to the photograph at page 48 will assist still further to make this explanation quite clear.

A ball some twelve inches from the ground could be back cut with more ease and safety than a ball two feet off the ground, and the danger of a catch is more remote.

Most of the power is imparted by the wrists, and after contact with the ball the bat should hit the ground directly afterwards. There is no long swinging movement as we find associated with the drive, but a short, quick wrist action.

Whilst the back cut is a delightful shot to watch, and may be the means of producing a great number of runs, I must emphasise that the most judicious care must be exercised in selecting the ball to back cut, and the method of execution.

LEG GLANCE

HERE again we are touching upon one of the beauty spots in cricket. To see a finished batsman executing dainty leg glances is certainly a lovely sight.

With a normal off field the men placed behind the wicket on the leg side are generally two, sometimes only one. A bowler cannot always pitch the ball exactly where he wishes, and occasionally along comes a ball pitched just outside the leg stump. Probably in a day's play you will not get very many, so it behoves you to take the fullest advantage of the loose ones you do get.

As with the drives and the defensive strokes, so, too, leg

glances may be played either forward or back. We will deal with the forward leg glance first.

Imagine a half volley pitched outside the leg stump in the direction of the batsman's pads. Here you have a ball inviting the forward leg glance. To make such a glance one really goes through exactly the same movements as when making an on drive, with very small variations. The right foot remains stationary; the left foot goes down the pitch, but slightly to the off side. Should the ball be allowed to go straight on without touching the bat, it would hit just the outer edge of the left leg provided that leg was in the correct position. Instead of swinging the bat at the ball in the manner indicated for an on drive, a leg glance is what the name implies—a glance. The full face of the bat cannot be utilised. The ball must be glanced, and to do this the face of the bat must be turned slightly towards the on side.

If the batsman intended a very fine leg glance close to the wicket-keeper, the face of the bat would be turned considerably, whereas if he intended to glance the ball squarer, and consequently near the square leg umpire, more of the full face of the bat would be used.

In making a leg glance, a batsman naturally seeks to evade any fieldsmen placed on the leg side. The placing of the field will automatically determine whether a fine leg glance is required or otherwise, and, of course, the batsman will endeavour to carry out his intentions accordingly.

When first practising a leg glance, the batsman should be satisfied with glancing the ball anywhere on the leg side. Once a reasonable state of perfection has been achieved in doing so, the art of placing a leg glance can be correctly cultivated.

As with the drives, the bat should meet the ball just before the bat has quite reached the perpendicular. If this practice is not carefully observed, the ball will have a tendency to fly upwards after passing the batsman. A slight flick of the wrists as contact is made will help to impart more speed to the ball, but this is scarcely necessary, unless one intends to deflect the ball considerably from its original course.

Obviously it would be foolish to attempt a forward leg glance from a ball pitched just short of a good length. From this ball we make use of the leg glance played by going back.

The same movements as those employed in making a back defensive stroke are used. The back foot is moved back towards the wicket, and slightly across in front of the wicket, whilst the left foot is brought across towards the right foot, and as described for a forward leg glance, the ball should hit the outer edge of the left leg if allowed to pass the bat.

The ball must again be glanced without quite using the full face of the bat as in making a forward leg glance, but there are just one or two little things which I would like to advocate.

The first is this. When playing a back defensive stroke you will remember I held my left wrist behind the handle of the bat. When making a leg glance by playing back I allow my left wrist to stay in front of the bat handle, because it makes the carrying out of the shot much easier. The bat is not held in a perpendicular position as when making a back defensive shot, but is allowed to move on after making contact with the ball. For this reason I find it easier to make a leg glance with the left wrist in front of the bat handle.

Greater control over this shot will probably be achieved by allowing the right hand to slip down the handle slightly.

With these two leg glances at your command, the whole of the area between square leg and the wicket-keeper should be amply covered, with the exception of the hook stroke, which I am now about to describe.

HOOK STROKE

SOMETIMES it is difficult to explain the difference between a hook stroke and a pull shot. There is a considerable difference of opinion. May I try to put it this way. You would think it quite natural to hear a man say: "Mr Brown hooked a ball right off his face round to fine leg." But it would sound out of place to hear: "Mr Brown hooked a ball from two feet outside his off stump." In the latter case the words "he pulled a ball from outside the off stump" would no doubt be more appropriate.

One generally speaks of pulling a ball to leg from a slow bowler, but with a fast bumping ball from an express merchant it is usually termed hooking the ball. For the purpose of demonstration I propose to confine the hook shot to that played from a rising ball pitched on the wicket to outside the leg stump.

Imagine a man of great speed to be bowling, and dropping the ball about half-way down the pitch. As a general rule that delivery would rise at least chest high by the time it reached the batsman.

The height to which the ball will rise after hitting the

pitch is always an uncertain quantity. For this reason, a batsman is practically forced to be in a position to play at any ball pitched on the stumps. So with a fast short-pitched ball on the wicket the batsman must be ready.

By standing in his original position and playing a defensive stroke, the danger of a catch in slips is at once evident should the ball lift to a dangerous height. By moving in front of his wicket to play a defensive shot there is the danger of physical injury should the ball rise higher than expected.

Without any doubt the safest and best method of dealing with such a ball (unless, of course, a concentrated leg field is packed) is to move inside the ball so that it will pass on the leg side of the batsman's body. Should it rise shoulder high, the nearest point of the batsman's body to the ball should be the left shoulder. So, then, to play a hook shot, move across and slightly backwards, and as the rising ball comes up towards your shoulder, swing the bat at the ball to lift it in the direction mid-way between square leg and fine leg. In swinging at the ball a pivot will be made of the right foot, and the batsman will automatically swing round on this foot after hitting at the ball, to finish up facing towards the leg side.

It is practically impossible, on account of the height to which the ball has risen from the pitch, to prevent hooking the ball into the air. Unless the leg field is packed the danger of being caught from such a shot is not very great, whilst a four is almost certain if one connects properly with the ball. To the high-pitched bumping ball without a leg field it is much safer to move towards the off, thereby allowing the ball to pass by the batsman on the leg side, than to adopt the opposite course of allowing the ball to pass on the off side of the batsman. A fast right-hand bowler is much more likely to make the ball veer towards the leg side than the off side unless the ball is new and he is making it swing away to the off. Any turn from the pitch by a bowler of pace will generally be from the off towards the batsman's body.

PULL SHOT

I HAVE a particular interest in and love for the pull shot. Having played my first few cricket matches on concrete wickets, and being slightly under the average height, I found it difficult to negotiate the ball slightly under-pitched with a straight bat. The resultant outcome of this was I was forced to employ a shot whereby I pulled the ball to the on side with a cross bat.

When I arrived in Sydney and commenced playing on turf I endeavoured to exploit this shot in the same manner. Now, a ball comes off a hard turf wicket faster than it does off a concrete wicket covered with matting, but it does not rise quite so high. Being inexperienced on turf I found it somewhat difficult to pull the ball with any precision. Immediately I was advised from all sides to cut this shot out. Many reasons were given, the principal one being it would get me out.

I did not feel like discarding a shot which helped me to make runs in the country, and set about practising my pull shot in an effort to adapt it to the changed conditions.

To pull a ball successfully there are several governing factors. The first is sound judgment in picking the right ball from which to attempt the shot. Without this judgment no player can hope to employ it successfully.

Very keen and quick eyesight is essential.

One must never attempt to pull a ball which is of good length or over-pitched; it is only the ball slightly under-pitched or short of a good length which can be efficiently pulled with any degree of safety. To the ball pitched on the wicket one cannot afford to miss, otherwise the wicket will be bowled down or an l.b.w. decision will result. When attempting to pull a ball pitched outside the off stump the chief danger lies in the possibility of pulling the ball on to the wicket, although by judicious placing of the feet this may be largely overcome. With a ball pitched outside the leg stump these dangers can be forgotten; they do not exist.

I have seen many players attempting to pull a ball to the on side somewhere between mid-on and square-leg. They have been able to do so with a reasonable amount of accuracy, but cannot make the shot without hitting the ball into the air, and this applies to quite a few international players. Invariably I have traced the cause to their grip of the bat.

My method of playing a pull shot is this. Move back and across with the right foot as the ball comes either towards the body or just on the off side of the body. Bring the bat across in an almost horizontal position, in a manner very similar to that used when making a square cut, with this difference. In square cutting a ball, the bat cuts across and against the line of flight, whereas in pulling a ball, the bat more or less follows the course or line of flight. I cannot see how it is possible to pull a ball, and at the same time use a straight bat, without hitting the ball into the air. By pulling a ball with a horizontal bat—or if you prefer to call it so, a cross bat—you have a smaller margin for error, but you also have the opportunity of keeping the ball along the carpet. Here is where I find the practical value of keeping my left wrist behind the bat handle as compared to the other method of allowing it to remain in front. By pulling a ball with the left wrist in front of the handle, the blade in its natural position will be turned slightly upwards. As a consequence, any pull shot made with the blade in that position must lift the ball into the air.

On the other hand, with the left wrist kept behind the bat handle, we find the blade at the moment of contact turned slightly downward, giving the natural result of hitting the ball down towards the ground. Unless the ball rises in the vicinity of chest high, I never find the slightest difficulty in keeping a pull shot on the ground. In fact, I never even think of hitting it up in the air. If I wanted to loft the ball, I would have to change my method of carrying out the stroke.

Suggesting once again the medium-pace bowler with an ordinary off field, the area between square-leg and mid-on is generally unguarded. In consequence a pull becomes an extremely profitable stroke against a bowler who is inclined to be generous in the matter of dropping a ball just short of a good length. In every instance, the ball should be hit with the utmost power at one's command, and every effort should be made to send it right to the boundary. On hard, fast turf the pull cannot be employed a great deal. On a slow, easy wicket, it will be found much more effective. A glance at the photograph at page 80 after reading this discourse on the pull shot should make you clearly understand every aspect I have been trying to explain.

A quick glance at a sketch of a cricket ground, and a general survey of the areas which would be covered by the various shots just described, would suffice to show you there is no portion of the field to which a ball could not be played, and on many occasions by two or three of those methods.

It is of course wise to practise your shots gradually and rather methodically. I am always a firm believer in practising to a set plan. There are moments in a cricketer's career when a little relaxation at the nets is perhaps more effective than assiduous concentration, but this should not apply to the learner, who should devote his energies firstly to improving his game.

As a general rule it is a comparatively simple matter to arrange at practice for any type of bowling against which a batsman particularly desires practice. There is always a man in charge of the practice nets, and I have yet to find one who would not meet my desires in this respect.

A short example will better illustrate what I mean. Supposing you are to play on Saturday against a team whose attack consists mainly of fast bowlers. Practice against this type of bowling during the week would naturally assist you to be prepared for Saturday's bowling. Should the principal bowlers in the opposition for the following Saturday be slow bowlers, practice during that particular week should be largely devoted to batting against slow types of bowling.

When a match is actually taking place, it is wise for batsmen to have even just two or three minutes at the nets before play is due to commence for the day, and if the opportunity arises it may be in his interests to have a further practice before his time comes to bat.

When leaving the pavilion to walk out to the wicket, the player generally finds he emerges from shadow into the sunshine. We all know the effect of this is to cause a slight reaction to the eyes, very slightly blurring the sight until the eyes have adjusted themselves to the brighter conditions. For this reason many players prefer to sit in the open, awaiting their turn to bat, rather than in a dressing-room. This, however, is not always convenient, due to the facilities at some grounds being most inadequate, but there is nothing to prevent a batsman walking slowly to the crease, and thereby giving his eyes an opportunity to adjust themselves.

At the same time I want to stress that there is a time provided for in the laws of cricket—two minutes between batsmen—and players should diligently observe this rule. If the incoming batsman crosses the outgoing batsman at the gate, the man about to go to the crease will always find plenty of time at his disposal, and yet find he is well within the time allotted.

On arriving at the crease the batsman naturally takes block, a subject upon which I have already entered into a little discussion. After block has been taken, and the position of same duly marked on the pitch, it behoves a batsman to make a very careful mental note of the position of every fieldsman. He is, of course, aware of the type of bowler entrusted with the attack at the moment. Bearing this in mind, the placing of the field should immediately be some sort of a clue as to the bowler's intentions. If all the men are on the off side, it becomes perfectly obvious the bowler has no intention of bowling outside the leg stump, and so on.

This observance of the field is of vital importance not only at the commencement of the innings, but throughout the whole of the time the batsman occupies the crease.

Careful mental note should be made of any peculiarities in the field placing which may suggest a certain trap being laid. For every change of bowling, and for every movement that is made in the positions of the fieldsmen, the batsman must carefully watch.

Having satisfied himself as to the positions of the fieldsmen and the type of bowling to be used, the batsman should bear in mind not only the type of bowler, but the state of the pitch. Many a batsman has been caught unawares by attempting a stroke before he had any idea of the pace of the wicket.

I can still vividly remember an experience I had in this regard which taught me a lesson I have never forgotten. It was my first match on the Sydney Cricket Ground with the New South Wales Eleven. We were playing against Queensland, and when I arrived at the wicket our captain was batting, and had the strike to a slow bowler. The first ball was of good length to which he played back, forcing the ball to mid-on for a single. It looked so easy, I attempted to do the same thing from the first ball I received. I entirely overlooked the all-important fact that I had just arrived, whereas my captain had been in some time, and was quite accustomed to the conditions. I duly attempted to play the stroke, but was so late that the ball hit the stumps long before my bat had reached the spot where I had intended to make contact with the ball.

The very simple truth was the wicket was considerably faster than I had anticipated, the ball therefore going through too quickly for me, and I thoroughly deserved to lose my wicket for having played what was at that stage an unsound shot, but there is nothing like experience for a teacher, and I have never forgotten.

Once accustomed to the light and the pace of the wicket, the batsman can often make shots it would be folly for him to attempt at the commencement of his innings.

Apart altogether from the wicket, one must consider also what use the bowler is making of the ball, whether he is spinning it off the pitch, whether he is fighting it or swerving it in the air, or whether all his efforts to do so are futile. Normally, it takes a very short time to observe these things. Once having done so, and provided the state of the match will allow, my idea of batting is to make attack the whole basis of the game.

I purposely say provided the state of the match will allow, because we all know there are certain circumstances wherein it would be foolish for a batsman to attack, but I am speaking now of the general policy to be adopted by the batsman. It has been, and always will be, my aim to score or attempt to score from every ball that is bowled to me, unless forced to play a defensive shot, or unless circumstances decree otherwise. A batsman may attempt to hit eight consecutive balls to the boundary, but not secure a single run. This may be due to faulty placing or excellent fielding, but it at least shows the right idea.

Think of the psychological effect upon the bowler if he can deliver ball after ball, pegging the batsman down so that he cannot score. It must give him an optimistic feeling. On the other hand, should you score even just a single from the majority of his deliveries he cannot help but lose some of his confidence. The moral effect upon the bowler is always there to a degree. With a bowler inclined to be faint-hearted, that effect is magnified considerably.

By advocating attack as the first method of defence I do not for a moment countenance wild, reckless hitting. Sound common sense must be used by every individual batsman. The best method of attack may be boundaries, and yet there are occasions when a series of singles would disorganise the bowler considerably more than boundaries.

These things a batsman must decide for himself, and he cannot possibly follow any rule of thumb.

Having surveyed the position, the batsman waits the delivery of the ball. As the bowler commences his run to the wicket so should the batsman totally forget all outside influences, and concentrate his whole attention upon that bowler. By paying strict attention to the arm and hand just prior to delivery, it is very often an easy matter to gain at least some idea of what type he intends delivery to be.

Any player who understands something of bowling realises the grip required and the delivery used when sending down an off break or leg break as the case may be; similarly, a swerve may be indicated. This anticipation of the bowler's intentions helps a batsman considerably in getting into position for the stroke.

Not only must the bowler's hand be followed, but at the same time it must be observed where he is delivering the ball from, a position close to the stumps or right out on the edge of the popping crease. The wisdom of this will be readily observed, for with a margin of nearly four feet to work in, such a difference may considerably alter the line of flight of a ball.

Once the ball has been delivered, there should be no other consideration than this—watch the ball. It is absolutely futile for any player to attempt to watch a fieldsman and the ball at the same time. His whole powers of concentration must be on that ball, and so far as it lies within his power to do so, he must watch it until the very moment it makes contact with the bat. In that simple phrase, "watch the ball", lies one of the most general causes of batting failures. The slightest tendency to take one's eyes from the ball after it has been delivered will ultimately, if not immediately, result in disaster.

It should be obvious to everyone that it is impossible to watch the positions of the fieldsmen when actually playing the ball. This, however, is where the value of making a mental note of the positions of the fieldsmen is realised. Without knowing where all the men are, it is impossible to place one's shots with any degree of accuracy.

What constitutes fast scoring? Not necessarily hard hitting in attacking the ball. There are not many fieldsmen who miss the ball when it is driven straight to them, neither is there any fieldsman living who can stop the ball which is driven out of his reach. The art of hitting boundaries lies principally in the power of the batsman to place the ball between the fieldsmen. Placing is one of the key-notes of skilful, scientific batting.

And again, placing the ball may not always mean hitting the ball to the boundary between two fieldsmen; it may be vitally important to disorganise a bowler's field. For instance, if the field is placed rather deep to cut off the boundaries, the wisest tactics may be to hit the ball gently so that easy singles may be run, and in this way swell the score very quickly.

By constantly placing the ball short of the fieldsmen, the opposing captain will probably find it necessary to reorganise his field to cut off the singles. The alteration he decides upon may leave the very opening you have been waiting for, and perhaps you can then proceed to drive the ball through the close-in fieldsmen to the boundary.

Both of the fielding captain's moves having been frustrated, he must naturally be called upon to think out some other scheme, and if he is in this position undoubtedly you have the upper hand for the time being. It is during these moments batsmen frequently help themselves, whilst the enemy is reorganising forces.

Perhaps the opposition has placed a strong off-side field, with scarcely anyone fielding on the on side. It is most unlikely you can attack the ball on the off side with such power and skill as to defeat his array of fieldsmen on that side.

On the other hand, two or three deft pulls to the on side will probably have the effect of causing an extra fieldsman to be brought across, and, of course, this means one less on

FORCING SHOT OFF BACK FOOT (see page 29)

SQUARE CUT OFF FRONT FOOT (see page 29)

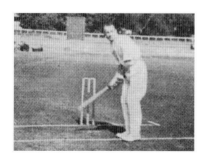 

SQUARE CUT OFF RIGHT FOOT (see page 29)

the off side, and may give you increased opportunities of scoring on that side.

All these things must be considered by the batsman as play progresses. There may even be an occasion when, with a strong cordon of close-in fieldsmen, the bowler has you slightly concerned about the possibility of giving a catch near the wicket. On such occasions the successful lofting of the ball into the outfield will very often speedily remove one or more of these dangerous in-fieldsmen.

When attempting any shot whereby the ball is intended to travel up in the air, the greatest care should be taken to make a safe hit. The ball mishit along the ground cannot be caught, but a ball mishit into the air always bears a sign to the fieldsmen, "Catch me."

Just as watching the ball is an essential, so is correct footwork; in fact, I have often heard it said of a young player, "he will make a great batsman, look at his footwork." There is no doubt that getting into the correct position to make a shot is half the battle.

There is a wealth of meaning in the term "getting into the correct position." At first glance it would seem to indicate just moving the right foot back when necessary for a defensive shot, and such like, but really it means more than that. At all times the batsman should endeavour to dictate to the bowler.

Naturally, a bowler frequently attempts to deliver a ball of such a length that the batsman will be in two minds as to whether he should play forward or back. By a combination of sound judgment of flight and correct footwork, the bowler's object in this regard may be very largely defeated.

To a ball pitched just short of a good length when the batsman is standing in his crease, it will be found quite short of a good length if he plays back to the full extent of the margin allowed by the distance from the batting crease to the stumps. To a ball just slightly overpitched, the batsman by playing forward may convert it into a half volley which can be easily driven. This phase of batting becomes more pronounced against slow types of bowling.

It is an extremely difficult thing to play against a correct slow bowler, who has command of flight and spin, by remaining in one's crease. He can pitch the ball on a given spot time after time until eventually you are trapped. By waiting for the right moment, and jumping down the pitch to convert what may have been a dangerous ball into a simple half volley or full pitcher, the bowler is forced to alter his length.

He will perhaps try and lure you into jumping down the wicket to one which drops short. In this respect, of course, he matches his wits against yours, but in forcing him to vary his length and flight, whether he wishes to or not, you stand a much better chance of forcing him to bowl more loose deliveries than would otherwise be the case.

Once a bowler loses his accuracy, and particularly a slow bowler, a great percentage of his effect is lost with it.

So, then, may I advocate, particularly to all budding cricketers, do not be afraid to leave your crease. I honestly think I have seen more men stumped by staying in their crease, playing forward, and dragging their toe over the line, than I have where men have gone yards down the wicket to meet the ball. Unquestionably, the man who can attack a slow bowler by jumping out to him when necessary has a tremendous advantage over the flat-footed batsman who continually remains in his crease. The illustration at page 64 shows the footwork required when jumping out to drive.

I have on previous occasions stated that if the ball is one to which the batsman should play forward, he can generally drive the ball. It is unsound to play forward to a ball unless the batsman can be certain of smothering any break or spin which may be imparted to the ball,

It is also unsound to swing the bat against any break which may be on the ball. May I clarify this by a little explanation.

Imagine a leg-break of good length pitched six inches outside the leg stump. The batsman with a cross bat swings at the ball in an effort to hit it to square leg. On the majority of occasions you will find the ball goes up in the air even if hit correctly, whilst if mishit it very often results in an easy catch close in.

On the other hand, to attempt to swing an off-break pitched in a similar position to square leg would be quite sound, as the ball is breaking in the same direction as the bat is moving, and there is very little danger of a mishit up in the air.

Once again common sense must dictate the player's efforts. If there were no fieldsmen whatever in the country it may be quite a justifiable reason to hit against the break. These things are always governed by circumstances, and I merely mention them as a general principle.

Another important phase in good batsmanship lies in the efforts of a batsman to shield a weaker partner when he may be in trouble.

Supposing A and B are batting, and C and D are bowling. Batsman A finds both bowlers easy to handle, batsman B can manage the bowler C but finds great difficulty in negotiating the deliveries of bowler D. The natural thing for batsman A is to take as much of the bowling of bowler D as he possibly can, whilst his partner, B, will of course assist him in his efforts.

Whilst such a thing comes under the category of good teamwork, I consider it is also part and parcel of the make-up of a really high-class batsman, whose art lies not only in making runs for himself but in assisting his team or the members of his team to add to their totals also.

In this respect, as always, it is necessary for a batsman to be guided by a spirit of unselfishness.

Perhaps owing to some misunderstanding between the batsmen it is obvious somebody must be run out. Of the two men batting together at the moment one is a great batsman, the other comparatively poor. The duty of the weaker batsman by his team is to sacrifice his wicket for that of the better player, even though it may not even be the weaker player's fault that the misunderstanding has occurred. Such an act may quite easily mean 100 runs to the batting side.

I cannot instill into your minds too strongly the team spirit. Unless the interests of the team are your first consideration then it would be better not to play at all.

Whether batting, bowling, fielding or doing a service to one's team mates off the field, the same thing applies.

BOWLING

IT would be presumption on my part to think I could write a chapter on bowling which embodies everything a bowler should know.

I have never been classed as a good bowler and never will be, and so from the very commencement I say quite frankly I am largely giving you a batsman's point of view of bowling, together with what knowledge of the art I have gained through watching, listening to, and playing with some truly good bowlers.

If there is one subject upon which all bowlers agree it is this: accuracy is the keynote of all bowling. In other words, the very first essentials are length and direction. The combination of the two gives accuracy.

Many times have I been asked the difference between bowling in Test cricket and the bowling in lower grades of cricket. I have always replied: "In ordinary cricket one receives an excellent ball occasionally and a lot of bad ones. In Test cricket one receives a bad ball occasionally and a lot of good ones." The real difference, then, is the higher the grade the greater the accuracy.

Let us take first of all the little fellow of tender age, in whom strength and stamina have not yet developed.

Whilst he can be taught all the essentials of bowling, it is folly to expect him to commence with a full-size ball bowling twenty-two yards. Even a man would be more accurate at a distance of ten yards than he would be at twenty yards. For the same reason a child would find it more difficult to cultivate accuracy, bowling the full length. Whether batting, bowling, fielding, or doing a service to one's team mates off the field, the same thing applies of the pitch, than it would if it were shortened for convenience to fifteen yards.

The tutors who have the moulding of a boy's cricketing future might well remember this when they first commence coaching. A cricket ball slightly smaller and lighter than regulation size can easily be procured, and the length of the pitch shortened to the required distance according to the age and strength of the boy.

As he grows older so may he gradually learn to bowl a yard or two longer, until eventually the full distance of twenty-two yards is reached.

If reasonable accuracy has been acquired over a shorter distance of say fifteen yards, then by working in gradual stages it should not be difficult for the boy to retain his accuracy by the time he is bowling full length, whereas a quick jump from fifteen to twenty-two yards might break down all the early training.

First of all the boy must decide, along with his advisers, what type of bowler he desires to be, that is, fast bowler, medium pace, or slow spin bowler. There are a few bowlers who, having commenced their cricketing careers bowling one type, have later changed to another type, but they are in a minority.

The average bowler cannot hope to meet with success unless he concentrates upon one particular style of bowling.

Having decided whether to become a fast bowler or slow

bowler, as the case may be, the next thing is to gauge the ideal run to the wickets for delivery of the ball.

The reason for this should be quite clear. A slow bowler does not need a long run, neither can a fast bowler hope to achieve great speed by a run of three or four yards.

Almost everybody has a natural run, and unless there is some radical fault therein it should be adhered to, though improved upon if necessary. The run to the wicket should be just long enough to achieve the object. For instance, a fast bowler would need to terminate his run just as he feels ready to impart the maximum amount of speed to the ball, and so on.

With every bowler an effort should be made to approach the wicket with an even, easy gait. Many a promising bowler has failed to improve beyond a certain standard because of an uneven, jerky run and delivery.

Before commencing his run for the delivery of any ball, a bowler should see that he invariably starts from the same place. He will thus start to run up in his own footsteps time after time.

Any variation that has to be made, such as I will mention later on, must be made in the last three or four strides.

By always running the same length a bowler should automatically overcome the bad and entirely unnecessary habit of bowling no-balls. No bowler can afford to deliver a ball from which he cannot hope to obtain the batsman's wicket. Rather, he must try to obtain a maximum efficiency from every delivery, and this cannot be obtained when no-balls are frequently called against him.

Presuming the boy has decided upon the type of bowling

he wishes to follow, and his run to the wicket, he must now devote his attention to acquiring accuracy.

What is meant by length and direction?

Length is the ability to pitch a ball practically on a given line drawn at right angles across the pitch. Controlled direction means being able to deliver the ball in line with a certain stump or other object, whenever desired. The two combined enable the bowler to pitch the ball on any given spot on the wicket and in line with any object at the same time.

Being able to bowl a good length does not mean bowling every ball of perfect length. The bowler may desire to overpitch one occasionally, or perhaps drop the ball shorter, as part of his scheme to outwit the batsman. However, for him to become a perfect bowler, it is necessary that he should be able to bowl whichever ball he desires whenever he wishes. I admit this to be almost impossible—it is merely the goal to be striven for.

That ball which we say is of good length, is generally regarded as the most difficult to play, and to define what is meant by a good-length ball, I would say it is a ball of such a length that it creates indecision in the mind of the batsman, who does not know whether he should play forward or back.

Under normal circumstances the average bowler naturally tries to deliver as many good-length balls as he possibly can, though, as previously mentioned, the state of the game may call for deliveries which, though not of a good length, are actually better under the circumstances than good-length balls would be.

Another important factor when defining a good-length ball which must not be overlooked, is this. A good-length ball from a fast bowler would be pitched shorter than a good-length ball from a slow bowler, and similarly would vary for all types of bowling.

The bowler must use considerable judgment in varying his length according to the type of batsman opposed to him. A tall player with considerable reach could make a half volley from the ball which would be of a good length to a very short batsman, and so on. Yet if a small player was very nimble at getting down the wicket to a slow bowler, that gentleman might be forced to alter his length slightly in order to prevent the batsman from leaving his crease.

Whilst mentioning all these things, they are really matters for a bowler's judgment. All I can do is to point out the facts and stress the need for bowlers to observe batsmen individually, not collectively.

In his initial endeavours to cultivate accuracy of length and direction, the lad should do so without making any effort to impart spin to the ball. Better to be an accurate bowler without spin than a spin bowler without accuracy.

If it is the desire to become a spin bowler, endeavour to impart spin to the ball gradually after a considerable degree of accuracy has first been obtained by the ordinary straight up and down method. It is a most difficult thing to impart a great deal of spin to a cricket ball and at the same time retain accuracy. For this reason I advocate a rather gradual process of cultivating spin.

No boy can hope to become a really first-class bowler without spending many hours in an effort to perfect his bowling. Like a billiards player who practises day after day on a table to hit a ball on a given spot, so must a cricketer practise day after day with some definite object in view.

There are really only two directions in which a ball may be made to break. One is with an off break, the other is with a leg break. Over spin or back spin also may be imparted to a ball, but they do not alter the line of flight after the ball has hit the pitch, whereas the others do.

OFF BREAK AND LEG BREAK

SO that there may be no misunderstanding of what is meant, may I be pardoned for endeavouring to make this somewhat clearer.

Imagine a right-handed bowler delivering the ball to a right-handed batsman. The first ball is pitched on the off stump and hits the leg stump; that is an off break. The second ball is pitched on the leg stump and hits the off stump; that is a leg break.

When an off break has been delivered, and the ball is in the air, it is spinning over from left to right. With a leg break, the reverse is the case, the ball spinning over from right to left. A ball to which over spin has been imparted would be spinning in the same direction as the ball is travelling, whilst back spin would mean the ball is spinning in the opposite direction to which it is travelling.

The grips employed by many bowlers vary considerably in delivering an off break, one of the principal reasons being that their hands are not of the same size, the man with a very large hand having an advantage over the man whose fingers are comparatively small.

Perhaps I could do no better than say, grip the ball in such a fashion that you can impart most spin to the ball as you deliver it in the required direction.

You will find in delivering an off break that the principal work is done by the index finger. I find it suits most players to have the first and second fingers a considerable distance apart when gripping the ball, for by this means more strain is put upon the index finger, and consequently more spin is imparted to the ball as it leaves the hand.

When a leg break is to be delivered, one really has to adopt a method entirely the opposite to what I have just advocated for an off break. In the case of a leg break, practically all the work and strain falls upon the third finger, whilst the index finger more or less occupies the position of a balancing or guiding finger. To put the strain upon the third finger it is necessary to have the second and third fingers a distance apart. A short reference to the photograph at page 64 will serve much better than any written explanation.

Exactly the same grip as that employed for a leg break may be used when bowling a ball to which over spin has been imparted. The entire difference between the two deliveries comes from a change in the position of the wrist just as the ball is delivered, which I will explain more fully a little later.

Back spin is caused, again, by a change in the position of the wrist, and the art of delivering what is known as a googly, or "bosie," is entirely due to the manipulation of the wrist. To emphasise this fact, I will add that by gripping a cricket ball in exactly the same manner five consecutive times, the bowler could in turn deliver an off break, a leg break, a "bosie," an over spin, and a ball to which back spin has been imparted. Naturally this grip is varied for better results, but that illustration should serve to impress upon you what an important part the wrist plays in bowling.

To some people the art of delivering a break ball comes easily. I find others have a lot of difficulty in getting the idea. To the latter may I devote just a few lines.

Take a cricket ball and grip it in the manner suggested for a leg break. Hold the ball in your hand in front of you with the palm of the hand facing upward, twist your hand and wrist quickly from right to left, at the same time spinning the ball with the fingers. This will give you some slight indication of the movement that will be required of the fingers and wrist when a leg break is actually delivered in practice.

Now just exactly what is a googly? I will try and make this a little clearer also. It is really an off break delivered with a leg break action, the intention of the bowler being to make the batsman believe by his actions he is delivering a leg break, whereas when the ball hits the pitch it is spinning in the opposite direction.

When a leg break is being delivered, the palm of the hand as the ball is about to leave the hand would be facing away from the bowler, in the direction of the batsman or towards the square leg umpire. When a googly is bowled it should be gripped in exactly the same manner as a leg break. In every possible way the bowler should endeavour to make the delivery of the "bosie" appear identical with that of the leg break. As well as being gripped the same, the ball is spun the same by the fingers, but the position of the wrist must be reversed so that the ball, as it leaves the hand, even though spun in the same manner by the fingers, will be turning in the opposite direction as it is propelled through the air.

As the ball is leaving the bowler's hand, instead of the palm of the hand facing the batsman, it will be found almost facing directly away from the batsman and behind the bowler. The ball then, instead of coming out of the front of the hand, comes out of the back of the hand up over the little finger and up over the wrist as it starts on its way down the pitch.

It is very difficult to explain this delivery, but I feel sure that readers will be able to follow what I mean if they take the trouble to follow these directions closely, remembering all the time that the position of the wrist is everything, and all these things can be demonstrated whilst standing perfectly still.

I have endeavoured to emphasise very strongly the position of the wrist relative to the bowling of a break ball.

You have already learnt that with exactly the same grip one may deliver different types of breaks and in the description of bowling a googly, readers should find the nucleus for learning how to bowl a ball to which over spin has been imparted.

You already have the position of the wrist for delivering a leg break and for delivering a "bosie". Take a position exactly midway between the two, the grip exactly the same as that for a leg break. At the moment of delivery the palm of the hand will be facing almost towards the ground. The back of the hand will certainly be facing upwards with the palm of the hand, if not facing the ground, then facing away from the batsman.

Delivered in this fashion the ball will be spinning at a very great speed in exactly the same direction as it is travelling, and obviously as it makes contact with the pitch it will gather additional speed.

To anyone with ambitions in the art of googly bowling, it will probably be advantageous to practise the over spin ball before really attempting the googly. The over spin is much easier to control, and not so hard to deliver.

FLIGHT AND SWERVE

IF I were a scientist, I would probably explain to readers the reason why a cricket ball will swing in a certain direction as it travels through the air. Not being a scientist, I will content myself with endeavouring to explain which way a ball will swing according to the spin imparted to it.

There are two common deliveries, which we call: (1) An outswinger. (2) An inswinger.

When the ball is new it will swing of its own accord, without any spin being imparted to the ball. Certain bowlers have the ability to make a ball swing much more than others, but generally the following will prove a true guide.

Take a ball and hold it in front of you with the seam running perpendicularly round the ball and pointing in the direction of the gully. Holding the ball in that position, deliver it perfectly straight and it will have a tendency to swing away in the direction of the slips. That is what we term an outswinger.

Holding the ball in the same fashion, turning the seam until it is pointing midway between square and fine leg, and delivering the ball straight when holding it in this position, the ball will veer towards the leg side, being what we call an inswinger.

By judicious arm and wrist movements the amount of swing can very often be increased or modified as desired.

Once the newness has gone, and the sheen has worn off the ball, the bowler generally finds it necessary to deliver what we call a spin swerve if he wishes the ball to change its course during flight.

The finest illustration I know of to demonstrate spin swerve is with a tennis ball. On account of its construction a tennis ball may be gripped more tightly than a cricket ball, and will respond much more quickly to any spin, but exactly the same principles apply to a minor degree with a cricket ball. If anyone wishes to test this theory, let him just do what I suggest.

Take a tennis ball. Grip it in the manner described for an off break very firmly. Throw the ball as hard as possible, at the same time imparting as much spin as you can to the ball (that is, off-break spin), towards a given object some thirty yards away. You will invariably find the ball will alter its course considerably from right to left, that being the direction taken by an outswinger. After a few throws you will probably be able to make that ball alter its course, not inches but feet, in even such a comparatively short space.

Adopt exactly the same method again, only on this occasion impart leg-break spin to the ball, and exactly the opposite effect will be obtained. The ball will alter its course from left to right. A cricket ball thrown in this manner would not illustrate what I am describing nearly so efficiently as a tennis ball will, but there you have the basis for delivering what is known as a spin swerve.

The slow medium-pace off-break bowler bowling into a nice wind always makes the ball drift away towards the off side of the batsman.

A leg-break bowler, bowling into the wind, will always find the ball drifting towards the batsman's legs.

By judicious control and usage of any such swing the bowler may increase his efficiency tremendously. For instance, if by delivering the ball towards the off stump it is continually drifting a foot outside the off stump, and the batsman is allowing the ball to pass, the bowler may need to alter his direction, delivering the ball just outside the leg stump so that it would drift back and eventually land on the wicket in a line with the stumps. In this regard, of course, he must use his own judgment, according to the conditions.

When a slow leg-break bowler is operating into a nice breeze, delivering the ball towards the middle stump, and it is carried outside the leg stump only to break in again towards the wicket, he is generally extremely difficult to play, whereas without this in-swing his deliveries would not be nearly so dangerous.

The swing of a ball through the air comes under the category of flight, but generally when we speak of fighting a ball we refer to a slightly different phase of bowling.

The non-striker need only have his bat within his ground as the bowler delivers the ball. Once the ball has been delivered he is then in position to "back-up."

Showing how the non-striker should "back-up" just after the bowler has delivered the ball. The yard or two gained by judicious backing-up will very often be the means of preventing a run out.

All reference to positions in the field are made in accordance with those marked on this diagram, which is set for a right-hand bowler bowling over the wicket to a right-hand batsman. The positions would automatically change for a left-hand batsman, or when ends were changed.

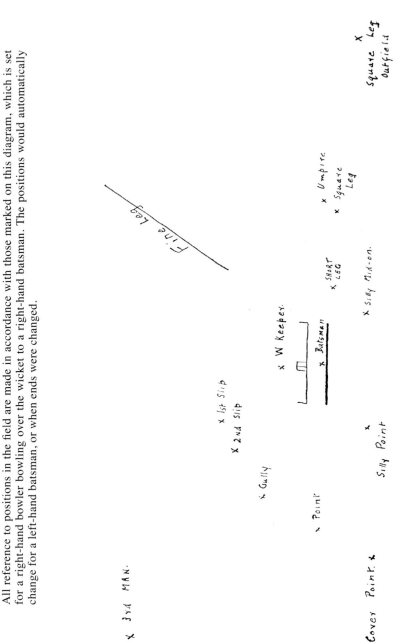

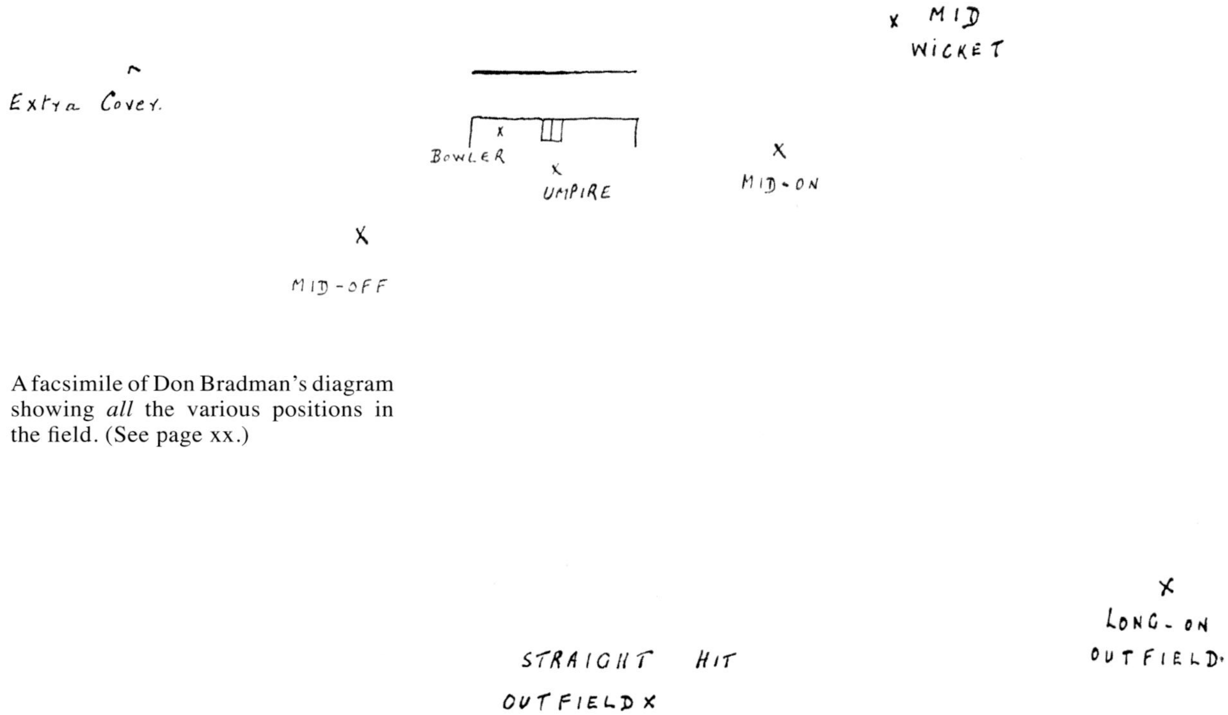

Extra Cover.

x MID
WICKET

x
MID-ON

x
MID-OFF

BOWLER
x
UMPIRE

A facsimile of Don Bradman's diagram showing *all* the various positions in the field. (See page xx.)

X
LONG-ON
OUTFIELD.

STRAIGHT HIT
OUTFIELD x

GRIP FOR THE
OUT-SWINGER

Notice the seam pointing towards
the slip fieldsman (see page 62).

GRIP FOR THE
LEG BREAK

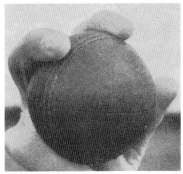

Note distance between 2nd and 3rd
fingers. The leverage for the spin
comes principally from the 3rd
finger (see page 58).

GRIP FOR THE
IN-SWINGER

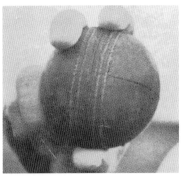

Notice the seam pointing towards
fine leg (see page 62).

LEG BREAK BEING
DELIVERED

(See page 59.)

LATE CUT (see page 32)

BACK LEG GLANCE (see page 34)

FORWARD LEG GLANCE (see page 34)

What is principally referred to as "variations of flight" is when a bowler makes a ball fall shorter than the batsman thought it would, or vice versa. This effect may be gained once again by the judicious use of spin. An exaggerated illustration can also be obtained in this regard by practising with a tennis ball.

The more over spin imparted to a ball, the quicker will it drop to earth. The more back spin that is imparted to a ball the greater the tendency for the ball to continue rising upward whilst it retains its velocity. Hence a slow leg-break bowler, by varying an over spin ball occasionally with a leg break, may cause the batsman to jump down the wicket only to find the ball dropping a foot or two shorter than he anticipated.

It should be readily understood from the foregoing explanations why variations of flight are mainly confined to slow or slow medium-pace bowlers. When the ball is travelling at any great speed variations in pace are quite possible, but fighting the ball becomes much more difficult.

Most cricketers are aware that it is generally wise for a slow bowler to bowl into the breeze. This is done so that he may obtain any advantage which is to be gained from the wind in the way of fighting the ball, whereas a fast bowler, assisted by a good breeze, will probably increase his pace as a result. Regarding changes of pace, all bowlers should endeavour to use their intelligence when bowling and not become mechanical instruments. Continually delivering ball after ball at the same speed and on the same spot will only play the batsman in, whereas variations of length and pace, wisely applied, will always keep him on the qui vive as to the next move.

When a bowler desires to deliver a ball slightly slower or slightly faster than is his custom, he should endeavour to deliver that ball in exactly the same manner as previously, in order that the batsman may receive no indication of any change of pace.

If the run to the wicket or the action is altered he will become suspicious and look for something unusual, but if your delivery is unchanged he may be caught unawares.

Some bowlers advise delivering the ball from a little farther back when wishing to bowl one a shade slower, but I do not think this is a wise principle. Although it may have the desired effect with regard to pace, it will probably, in addition, cause the bowler to become slightly erratic with his length. Obviously, if his feet are some inches farther from the batsman he must need to deliver the ball that much farther down the pitch, otherwise the delivery will be slightly short pitched, and thereby possibly his objective will not be gained. Consequently, I would advise deliveries being made from approximately the same distance, any variations in pace to be made from that spot.

USE WIDTH OF BOWLING CREASE

HOW many bowlers do we see running up to deliver ball after ball in exactly the same place, without thinking for a moment of utilising the space which is available to them?

From the edge of the stumps to the outer edge of the

bowling crease there is a distance of nearly four feet, which the bowler is perfectly entitled to use, and should use, to his own advantage.

By delivering one ball with the feet and body very close to the stumps the ball will be delivered almost perfectly straight, but if the feet are out on the edge of the bowling crease the ball will be travelling at a slight angle to the batsman. This angle may be only small, and yet it may considerably assist the bowler, according to the type of delivery. Consequently I would advise all bowlers to take every advantage of the width of the bowling crease to assist them in their efforts to get the batsman out.

Take the case of a man bowling round the wicket. We will say a right-hand bowler. He may deliver a ball from the edge of the bowling crease, and at the moment of delivery the ball may be two yards to the right of the stumps. It pitches of good length on the centre stump, but it carries on without turning in the slightest degree and misses the off stump, on account of the angle from which the ball was delivered.

Exactly the same ball delivered with a slight off break pitched on the middle stump and of good length will turn after hitting the pitch, probably going directly towards the middle stump after leaving the pitch, the amount of spin on the ball being approximately sufficient to counteract the angle from which the ball was delivered. This is why many bowlers deliver the ball from round the wicket when they are turning the ball off the pitch. It assists them to obtain l.b.w. decisions.

I have met many people who think it is difficult for a

bowler to obtain an l.b.w. decision when bowling round
the wicket, but that is not the case. So long as the conditions
applying to l.b.w. decisions are fulfilled, the umpire must
give the batsman out whether the bowler is bowling over or
round the wicket.

When discussing variations of length it may be wise to
point out that a good length ball today may not be a good
length ball tomorrow. It depends largely upon the state of
the wicket. I learnt my cricket on a concrete pitch, which
is, of course, the same from one year's end to the other, but
on turf the characteristics of the pitch may vary a good deal
even in one day.

When the wicket is slow and easy the bowler must
generally pitch the ball a little farther up, otherwise the
batsman will be able to step back and play him comfortably,
whereas on a fiery wicket the bowler may be able to drop
his length slightly. At all times a slow bowler needs to pitch
the ball farther up than a fast bowler, whilst a medium-pace
bowler comes in between.

In the art of bowling a great deal depends upon
concentrating certain types of bowling against varying
types of batsmen. Let me give you an outstanding example.
Presuming the wicket to be a bowler's wicket after rain,
one left-handed and one right-handed batsmen are batting
together. Two bowlers of the same type are bowling, one
being left-handed and the other is right-handed. To the
right-hand batsman the left-hand bowler will most likely
prove very difficult, spinning the ball away towards slips,
whereas the right-hand bowler will have the left-hand
batsman in difficulties for the same reason. Obviously the

bowlers should make every effort to see that each of them bowls against the batsman whose wicket he is most likely to obtain. The right-hand batsman will, of course, try to get the strike against the right-hand bowler, an end to which his partner should assist him, but it is the bowler's job to try and prevent such a thing happening. It becomes a battle of wits between the players.

We frequently see a certain batsman who is uncomfortable when facing a certain bowler. Under these circumstances, that bowler should be given every opportunity of obtaining that batsman's wicket at the earliest moment.

When a new batsman arrives to commence his innings, it is only natural that he wants to secure his first run, and so get off the dreaded "duck". Bowlers should always make a special effort to prevent the batsman securing his first run. The longer he is at the wickets without scoring, the more unsettled he will very often become, and there are occasions when the batsman will make some unsound stroke trying to secure that first run, and so lose his wicket.

In the same way, we find occasionally one batsman well settled when a new player comes in, and the former will endeavour to take the strike for a few balls to give his partner a better chance. It is the bowler's job to prevent this, and so attack the incoming batsman as quickly as possible.

In certain circumstances it often pays to give a batsman one run to get the opportunity of bowling at the weaker partner. Too much emphasis cannot be given to the theory "set a field and bowl to it." Playing in minor matches, it is customary to find an orthodox field set and the bowler, having no plan of attack, bowling rather inaccurately. When playing in the higher grades of cricket, against men who understand cricket, and who have made a study of it, we find close attention has been paid to the placing of the field for different types of bowling. When an off field has been set, the batsman is very surprised if he receives a ball pitched outside the leg stump. This aspect of cricket is particularly noticeable with regard to the Englishmen, even in County matches at home, with bowlers who are well below Test match standard. They are extremely difficult to score from because they invariably set a well-placed field and bowl to it. No matter whether the bowler is highly proficient in his art or a comparative novice, he can still try to think out ways and means of disposing of the batsman, and there should be no need for me to point out the fallacy of setting an off field and bowling outside the leg stump, or vice versa. Nevertheless, let me again stress this fact—"set a field and bowl to it."

This is, of course, a general principle, and every bowler will use his own judgment. If he thinks it wise occasionally to deliver a ball which is not in conformity with his field, in an effort to bring about the dismissal of the batsman, well and good, and of course it should be almost unnecessary to point out that a different field in some slight degree will probably be required for each batsman.

There is scarcely any player who has not some weakness or some particularly strong point. The bowler should realise immediately where the strength and weakness lie, and place his men so that the batsman may be lured either into a false feeling of security or find his pet strokes covered, thereby forcing him to attempt other scoring shots in order to swell his total.

I can remember a player who scored fours with monotonous regularity for several matches, with magnificent cover drives. No effort was made to block this stroke, and consequently he went along his merry way picking up the runs in that spot match after match. The next time I saw this player in action, a concerted effort was made to prevent him scoring from this shot both by the method of bowling and the placing of the field, with the result that his subsequent performances fell to a considerably lower level, and so it is with most batsmen.

No matter how proficient they may be, the success of their efforts may very often be minimised considerably by the whole-hearted co-operation of bowlers and fieldsmen.

UMPIRES

THESE rather unfortunate gentlemen seem to be in the unhappy position of always receiving abuse, but seldom the plaudits. If they do their job conscientiously, and 100 per cent efficiently, it still does not mean they will be regarded as satisfactory, because I have repeatedly seen an umpire give a perfectly correct decision only to be roundly condemned by someone who thought he knew better, even though the latter was not in a position to judge, and probably had in addition an infinitely smaller knowledge of the game.

My view regarding umpires is this. Somebody must be in charge of the game. Everybody admits the necessity for authority, and umpires are appointed to carry out their duties to the best of their ability. If they do so, it does not behove us to criticise, unless their decisions are not in conformity with the rules.

In the majority of cases, particularly when we come to consider the highest classes of cricket, these umpires are men with ability and a very full knowledge of the subject.

When a decision has to be given by the umpire for l.b.w. or a catch, or whatever the case may be, it is rarely we find a decision given which is at variance with the laws of cricket. In the majority of cases the decision is one to be decided "in the opinion of the umpire."

His opinion may differ from that of the bowler or the batsman, but it cannot alter the decision, and I have not yet found an umpire in a game of any importance who was biased or deliberately gave a wrong decision.

When a batsman is given out l.b.w. it is his duty to accept the umpire's decision immediately, and without question, irrespective of whether the decision is right or wrong. The player who hesitates at the crease and tries to convey that he is dissatisfied with the decision, immediately shows himself in the light of a bad sportsman. Such actions will not improve his reputation, neither will they alter the umpire's decision.

I always mention one thing when discussing this aspect of cricket. When given not out after an l.b.w. appeal, no batsman ever attempts to convey the impression that he was out, and should have been given out. Therefore, when the reverse happens, why not play the game? It will even itself up in the end.

In the whole of my first-class cricketing career, I can remember only four decisions in which my opinion was contrary to that of the umpire. Twice I thought I was out, but was given not out; twice I thought I was not out, but was given out; and so with all other players throughout their careers. They will undoubtedly find in the end the scales balanced evenly.

If the umpire does his job perfectly, very few people think for a moment of bestowing a word of praise upon him. They merely say he did his duty, or he did what he should have done, but I think we owe a greater debt than that to our umpires. They have an unenviable position. It is part of our duty to assist them with their work, and endeavour at all times to make their task of giving correct decisions as light as possible. No effort to sway an umpire's jurisdiction by unfair suggestion should be condoned.

Whilst on the subject of officials it might be wise to add

a word of advice for the youngsters in regard to selectors. When a team is picked, there can only be eleven players. Somebody must be left out who thinks he should have been in. That person should always take his omission cheerfully, and it would do him, and everybody else, much more good if his attitude was one of wishing the other members of the team good luck, than if he voiced his disapproval of the selection, and showed some antagonism towards those selected in his stead.

These little things are really big things in the end, and they are vital cogs in the wheel which should run smoothly in the cricket world, wherein the characters of so many men of the future are moulded. There is no other game having such a vital effect on the character as cricket, and the more the high ideals of the game are cherished, and the more players endeavour to live up to them, the better it will be both for the game and its participants.

FIELDING

THE first duty of a fieldsman is to go wherever his captain instructs him. If the captain says, "George, take mid-off," it is not sufficient for him to go to mid-off and presume he is in exactly the position which the skipper intended him to occupy, but it is his duty to endeavour to ascertain that he does occupy the correct position. If the fieldsmen would only try to remember how much more the captain has to think about than they themselves, perhaps they would do more to assist him in his work than the majority of fieldsmen do at the present day.

Once the field has been set, most captains make a careful survey of the men, and these fieldsmen should see to it that they observe everything their captain does. Likewise, each and every fieldsman should instantly obey the commands of the skipper, and move speedily if any alteration in the field is required.

For a man to take up his correct position in the field at the outset is not sufficient. He must move to exactly the same spot on every occasion, unless instructed otherwise, allowing, of course, for changes of bowlers and batsmen.

During the course of the play a captain may require one of his men to move, not a great deal, but perhaps three or four yards in a certain direction, having some scheme in mind to outwit the batsman. Obviously, it would be unwise for the batsman to be made palpably aware of what was going on. The fieldsmen should carefully observe the captain, therefore, at very short intervals right through the match ready to receive and obey his commands.

It is somewhat difficult to lay down set laws which must be followed by the various fieldsmen. Men in different positions should act according to the dictates of that position. Take, for example, men who are stationed in such places as slips, silly point or short leg. As a general rule, they do not anticipate having to run after a ball, but they must at all times be wide awake for a catch which may come to them at any moment. For this reason they should study the prospect of getting a catch rather than the prospect of saving runs.

What, then, is the best way for fieldsmen in such positions as these to prepare themselves for the ball which might come their way at the most unexpected moment? The first thing is to be comfortable and well balanced, so that movements may be made with equal speed either to the right or the left. The weight should be equally distributed on the two feet (which should be some distance apart, this distance to be regulated by the comfort the individual acquires thereby), so that the fieldsmen is able to spring towards the ball coming toward the extremity of his reach on either side. Equal care must be given to see that one is prepared both for the low, skimming ball and the one which might pass overhead. For this reason it is unwise to get too far down on one's haunches or to stand very erect. The happy medium will generally prove the most beneficial.

With such positions as cover, mid-off, or the outfield, circumstances are almost entirely reversed. Whilst there is always the possibility of the catch coming their way, every one of these fieldsmen will be called upon to save runs more frequently, and will also, no doubt, get an opportunity of running a batsman out here and there. Saving runs, and running batsmen out, depend primarily upon two factors (apart, of course, from the sureness in picking up and the accuracy of returns, both of which are at all times essential). The two factors I refer to are anticipation and speed off the mark in moving to the ball.

Anticipation is more or less a natural gift. Some players are born with anticipation, but to the man to whom Nature has not been quite so kind, there is always the consolation in the knowledge that by keenness, enthusiasm, practice, and concentration, he will probably be able to acquire a sense of anticipation which will lift him out of the rut of ordinary fieldsmen. This sense of anticipation naturally assists any fieldsman very largely to gain speed in moving to the ball, but another little hint might also prove valuable here.

Take two foot runners of equal speed: one is made to start flat footed, whilst the other is allowed a walking start. If they were both on the mark as the gun went off, the man who was flat footed would be well behind at the end of the first ten yards. I would then advise the man fielding at some distance from the wicket to commence moving towards the batsman just as the bowler is about to deliver the ball.

Not only will this primary movement help to cut off runs, but in the event of a catch going up in the air it will, as a consequence, assist in the same manner to get to that ball more speedily.

This idea of moving as a bowler delivers the ball cannot possibly be followed by every fieldsman. How ridiculous would it look if silly point started to walk towards the batsman as the ball was delivered, or if the slips started moving up. These methods which I advocate to gain a flying start must be confined to those men who occupy suitable positions, making it advantageous for them to move up as the ball is delivered. At the same time such movements should be made quietly, for in no way must the attention of the batsman be distracted. Obviously it would not be fair to him otherwise.

The exact positions of all the fieldsmen in the vicinity of the wicket are directly controlled by the captain. For the man in the outfield the captain will very often merely indicate the direction in which he wishes the player to go, but some fieldsmen appear to be in doubt as to whether they should always field right on the boundary or some yards inside. In this connection, my own experience has been that the ideal position for an outfield to occupy is approximately five yards inside the boundary line. May I explain the reason why?

I say it is impossible for a batsman to hit a ball up in the air which will fall inside the boundary (in a direct line between the batsman and the outfield), which could not be caught by the fieldsman even though he was standing five yards inside the boundary when the ball was struck. On the other hand, he could definitely catch a ball five yards closer to the batsman than would be the case were he to stand right on the boundary line, in the event of a ball being skied and falling short.

Even when running round the boundary in an effort to cut off a four, I always like to be two or three yards inside if it is possible to remain there and still save the boundary shot. It gives one more freedom and a little room in which to move.

Perhaps, some players will say, if it is wise to stand five yards inside the boundary, why not make it ten? I would point out that there is a limit to the distance an outfield can come in. He can always move forward much faster than he can go back, and one cannot very well be an outfield and an infield at the same time. Just these five yards in from that boundary fence may also make the difference between a safe two and a possible run-out.

There is a tremendous amount of skill and thought behind a good fielding combination. Personally, I think it is an absolute treat to watch eleven players of outstanding ability using all their skill and intelligence when fielding, realising, as they should, how important fielding really is to a team. Every player should take a keen interest in fielding. It does not matter whether he is the star batsman, the star bowler, or just an ordinary player, one little slip on his part in the field may lose a match. Every man should concentrate on bringing his fielding up to a high standard of perfection.

Apart from the ability to stop and catch a ball, fieldsmen should always be awake to the possibility of running one of their opponents out, and when the opportunity arises should make an effort to bring about such an occurrence.

As a general rule, when a ball is hit to a man in the outfield, unless it goes reasonably straight to him, there should be a possibility of scoring two runs from the stroke. But if the outfield dashes in so that the batsmen on turning see that a second run is impossible owing to the speed with which the fieldsman reached the ball, they will, if they are wise, be content with the single and stay where they are. Rushing to a ball does not bring about run-outs, unless there has been a misunderstanding between the batsmen, or their judgment has been very much astray. On the other hand a run-out may sometimes occur entirely due to the judgment and strategy of the fieldsman. Always have in the back of your mind this thought: "If an opportunity for a run-out comes my way I must not miss it."

Presuming the ball is hit into the outfield, where there is a certain single and a possible two in the shot, what should the fieldsman do? I would say, move very fast towards the ball, and by judgment endeavour to be just so far from the ball when the batsmen turn for their second run that they will be undecided whether to attempt this second run or not. If they attempt to run, immediately he sees them doing so, the fieldsman should redouble his efforts to get that ball back to the wickets at lightning speed. He must first of all make sure he gathers the ball cleanly. It is not a bit of use trying to throw the ball back to the wicketkeeper until you have got it. Having the ball gathered cleanly, the next essential is a correct return. It may be necessary to throw at the stumps; if so, well and good. However, supposing the batsman is a long way out and there is plenty of time for the wicketkeeper or a fieldsman to take the ball and still run the batsman out, then it is futile to take the chance of hitting the wicket and probably spoil everything.

When it is necessary to return the ball to another fieldsman for the purpose of securing a run-out, endeavour to return it to him so that he will be able to take the ball about stump high just a few inches either side of the wicket.

HOOK (see page 37)

JUMPING OUT TO DRIVE—1 (see page 50)

JUMPING OUT TO DRIVE—2 (see page 50)

PULL SHOT (see page 39)

FIELDING—1 (see page 75)

FIELDING—2 (see page 75)

The men in the outfield generally get their opportunities for a run-out when a second run is being made. With the men closer in, such as mid-off and cover, they very often get their opportunities when the first run is being attempted. With these latter fieldsmen a quick dash to the ball is more often required and a different kind of strategy must be employed. Whereas the outfield tries to lure the batsman to his doom by making him imagine a second run is safe, the cover fieldsman may find it advisable to allow two or three possible run-outs go by in an effort to lull the batsman into a sense of false security, so that he will ultimately attempt a run which will prove impossible, when the fieldsman senses his opportunity.

What a wonderful asset it is to a cover field to be able to throw the ball from an underarm position without what we term "winding up." Run-outs more often occur by inches than yards, and inches mean fractions of a second. By fielding a ball and throwing it with the one movement the vital fractions of a second are gained, and therein lies the difference between a great fieldsman and just a good fieldsman.

When the ball is coming side on, or the player is forced to run at an angle to pick the ball up, it is mostly a case of get to the ball and pick it up as fast as you can before worrying about the throw, but where the ball is travelling in a direction almost straight towards the fieldsman, might I suggest what I consider to be the best method of fielding the ball and returning it with a maximum of speed and accuracy. In making these suggestions I am disagreeing with another international player who recently wrote a book, and whose method was entirely the opposite to what I am about to suggest, but I can merely leave it to my readers to judge for themselves who is right.

Let a man go out on to any cricket oval and practise this method of fielding a ball, and I am sure he will find it easy to learn, besides being advantageous to his fielding. I will try to describe as accurately as possible what is in my mind.

We will presume the ball has been thrown or hit along the ground directly towards me, and I am moving towards the ball. I am of course a right hand thrower. When within a few steps of the ball I try to regulate the length of my steps, so that I will be able to pick the ball up off the ground at the very moment which is suitable to me. The ball will not regulate its speed according to my run, so I must regulate my run according to the speed of the ball. I try to field the ball with both hands, some six to twelve inches in front of and slightly to the right of my right toe. If I failed to gather the ball it would pass some three inches to the right of my right toe. As I pick the ball up from the ground the entire weight of my body is on my right foot, but is just about to be transferred to the left foot. As my weight is transferred from the right foot to the left foot, so does my right hand go back into position to throw. Then as the ball is actually being thrown, so is the weight entirely thrown on to the left foot. If these directions are followed closely you will find not a moment will be lost in gathering the ball and returning it.

One need not stop running, although it may be advisable to slacken one's speed slightly in order to ensure accuracy in fielding the ball. Also, you can easily visualise how, by this method, the ball need not be thrown over arm. It is more of a round arm throw, and no preliminary "winding up" is necessary in the slightest degree. If any of my readers doubt the wisdom of this method let them try the opposite method of picking the ball up whilst the weight is on the left foot. It must be immediately obvious that two more steps are necessary before the ball can be thrown in the proper manner. Just that one extra step might make the difference of a hundred runs to the opponents.

Of course, the method I have advocated is the one which I endeavor to use when trying to run out a batsman. If there is no possible chance of obtaining a run-out, and speed in gathering and returning the ball is of no importance then greater care may be taken to see that the ball is effectively stopped and cleanly gathered. For instance, the fieldsman may deem it wise to stop and put his feet together, fielding the ball with both hands as it comes directly towards him, and directly between his feet.

When a hard return to the wicketkeeper is necessary, and the fieldsman has good control in his throw, he should endeavor to return the ball on the full. If this is not possible (perhaps owing to the distance of the throw) then endeavor to make the ball reach the wicketkeeper (or other fieldsman as the case may be) on the first bounce. Should it reach the wicket on the second bounce or running along the ground I need scarcely point out how much harder it is for the recipient to gather the ball cleanly.

It may also be wise to add a caution especially for the younger players, whose keenness may surpass their knowledge. If no run-out is possible, and if there is no occasion to return the ball hard to the wicketkeeper or bowler, then do not do so. I have frequently seen fieldsmen adopt this practice, sometimes unintentionally, sometimes with the desire to show onlookers what a great arm they possess, but invariably the unfortunate person receiving the ball has to take a very hard blow on the hands which is entirely unnecessary.

The wicketkeeper, having the protection of a pair of gloves, is better able to take a return from the field than the bowler. For this reason I would advise always returning the ball to the wicketkeeper unless the person returning the ball is reasonably close to the bowler, when the ball may be returned to him with accuracy and without any great speed.

I would also like to emphasise how necessary it is at all times to assist the bowler to conserve his energy throughout each day's play. At twelve o'clock the bowler may be fresh and the match in favour of the fielding side, but at five o'clock the star bowler may be tired and the match in favour of the batting side. It is at this juncture the fieldsmen may reflect upon how they allowed that bowler to chase a hit to the boundary, or how they returned the ball badly to him, making him strain to reach it or to bend over to pick it up.

These things sound mere trifles, but when it comes to a hard day's toil under strenuous conditions they are really important matters.

The last portion of this chapter on fielding I will devote to the question of backing up, which I am sorry to say is most noticeably absent in a considerable number of even our first-class games.

It is all very well to take it for granted the wicketkeeper will stop the ball when it is returned to him from the field, or a fieldsman will stop a hard drive just because it happens to be hit straight towards him, but we cannot afford to take these things for granted. One must be certain. As this is practically impossible, the next best thing is always to move behind the man who is about to stop the ball, so that in the event of him missing it by some piece of bad fielding or some mishap you will have done the right thing and will be there to retrieve his mistake.

I know it is very easy to stand still and watch somebody else rush to cut off a stroke, but self should be only a secondary consideration to the interests of the team as a whole.

When a match is lost by one run or one wicket, how often is the blame attached to the unlucky individual who happened to make the last mistake that occurred in the match. Actually, had some other player done his job properly three hours before there may never have been the opportunity of a mistake at the finish, the match having been won comfortably long before.

It is not the mistake in the last half hour which necessarily matters. The mistake which is made in the first five minutes might be ten times more important, but because of the situation of the match the earlier mistake is passed over without comment.

RUNNING BETWEEN WICKETS

RUNNING between wickets calls for a wonderful amount of judgment on the part of the batsmen concerned. Experience, too, plays a big part. Running with the same man as a partner on numerous occasions, so that a complete understanding is reached, is a wonderful asset, but there are also many basic principles which even bad runners could follow to the betterment of their own play.

As a youthful cricketer I was regarded as a bad runner between wickets. In country cricket this is an outstanding fault. One rarely finds in any country centre players who have a good knowledge of this particular branch of the art of cricket. No doubt my early associations with men who were not considered experts in running allowed me to get into bad habits from the start.

I can still picture vividly a short tour which was undertaken by a prominent player with a team of picked representatives, in which team I was fortunate enough to be included as a member. Also among the party was a batsman renowned as one of the finest runners between wickets in the whole of Australia. We played seven matches on that trip, and in each game an effort was made to enable me to be at the wickets at the same time, the object being for him to coach me in the art of running between wickets. The scheme did not always come off, particularly in one match when I was clean bowled first ball for a duck, but on a few occasions we were fortunate enough to be together for some time, and the experience I gained proved invaluable.

Twice I was run out, and once my partner was run out, but fortunately the games were not important, and the lessons which I learnt thereby helped me considerably in later years.

As a general guide, the accepted rule is that the striker shall call for a shot in front of the wicket, whilst the non-striker shall call for a ball which goes behind the wicket.

That is only a guiding principle, and cannot be followed on every occasion, but it will at least serve as a useful basis from which to commence.

Take for example such a case as this. The striker drives a ball to the covers and calls for a run. The non-striker, getting a bad start, sees that it is impossible for him to reach his crease at the other end. It is far better for him to say "no," thereby enabling the striker to regain his crease, rather than carry on with the run only to be run out just for the sake of obeying his partner's call. Of course, this is providing he can call "no" in sufficient time to enable his partner to return to the crease.

There are a hundred and one little ways whereby the two batsmen may co-operate with one another.

Presuming the ball to be glanced down to fine leg on the fence, it would be the non-striker's call. As he passes the striker in the middle of the pitch the non-striker should quietly inform him of the possibilities in the stroke by say-ing "one only," "possible two," "probable three," or in some way give the striker an indication of what he thinks the stroke is worth. Presuming he said as they passed "possible two," the striker would realise that by getting to the bowler's end and turning quickly he might gain the second run. Consequently he should make the turn speedily for the second and commence running immediately.

By the time the non-striker has reached the striker's end, he will be in a position to tell whether the stroke is now worth two or not. If he judges "yes," he will allow the striker to continue running for the second run, but if he judges "no" it would be his duty immediately to inform the striker of the danger, and so enable the striker to remain at the bowler's end.

No matter what part of the field the ball travels to, the batsmen can invariably help one another by guiding calls as they pass in the middle of the wicket.

There are so many other considerations also.

Batsmen immediately pick out those fieldsmen who can throw hard and accurately, and they unerringly pick out those men who cannot throw. It is infinitely safer to run when the ball is only forty yards away in the hands of a bad thrower than to run when the ball is sixty yards away in the hands of a skilful player with a powerful return.

If two batsmen commence running whilst a fieldsman still has the ball on the edge of the boundary, then they must be very slow runners if they cannot beat his return to the wickets, no matter how good he may be.

Skilful running very often disorganises fielding combinations, or upsets the bowlers' and captain's plans. When two batsmen do not take advantage of short singles, they enable the captain to place his fieldsmen that much farther away from the wickets, and so give them a much better chance of stopping the hard shots. But if no opportunities are lost in running short ones, the fielding captain must make some effort to prevent these runs being obtained. Perhaps he will bring the field in closer, only to see the ball being driven through them to the fence.

Occasionally we find a batsman who hesitates to run when the ball is hit softly, and who wants to go immediately he has connected with a hard drive. This, of course, is entirely the reverse to what he should do. A ball hit softly and travelling slowly towards a fieldsman takes longer to reach him, and takes longer to gather and return to the wickets, than a ball which is driven hard and is travelling faster.

With a hard shot travelling in the vicinity of an infieldsman, there is an infinitely greater risk in running than when a similar shot is made with less speed.

No matter what happens, always remember there are two batsmen at the wickets. Not only must your wicket be protected, but your partner's wicket, too. He may even be a better batsman than you are, and in that case it is more important from a team point of view that, if necessary, your wicket should be sacrificed rather than that of your partner.

For the non-striker to back up is another great aid to good running. You will find two photographs on this at page 64—the first indicating how the non-striker should be just before the bowler delivers the ball, the second showing his position just after the delivery. Notice the distance from the crease is a little over a yard. Thinking back, don't you remember a man being run out by less than this distance?

And so, dear readers, I will leave you with just a few final remarks. This book has been written mainly because of the requests of numerous young players, and not through a desire on my part to become a writer.

The ideas I have endeavoured to convey herein are meant primarily for the youths who have their cricket careers in front of them.

Very few can ever become outstandingly successful, but one and all can follow the paths trodden by characters of renown in the cricket world.

Play the game wholeheartedly, with spirit and zest, and play to win, but, irrespective of the outcome, always treat your opponents as you would have them treat you, and play it as a sport. In other words, play cricket in the fullest meaning of the term.

DEFINITION OF CRICKET

by Sir Frederick Toone

IT is a science, the study of a lifetime, in which you may exhaust yourself, but never your subject. It is a contest, a duel or melee, calling for courage, skill, strategy, and self-control.

It is a contest of temper, a trial of honour, a revealer of character. It affords a chance to play the man and act the gentleman. It means going into God's out-of-doors, getting close to nature, fresh air, exercise, a sweeping away of mental cobwebs, genuine recreation of the tired tissues. It is a cure for care, an antidote to worry. It includes companionship with friends, social intercourse, opportunities for courtesy, kindliness and generosity to an opponent. It promotes not only physical health, but mental force.

STATISTICAL RECORD OF DON BRADMAN'S CAREER

	Matches	Innings	N.O.	H.S.	Runs	Average	Centuries
All First-Class Matches	234	338	43	452*	28067	95.14	117
All Matches in Australia	142	218	25	452*	18230	94.45	76
All Matches in England	92	120	18	334	9837	96.44	41
All Test Matches	52	80	10	334	6996	99.94	29
Tests v. England	37	63	7	334	5028	89.78	19
v. England in England	19	30	4	334	2674	102.84	11
v. England in Australia	18	33	3	270	354	78.46	8
All Tests in Australia	33	50	6	299*	4322	98.22	18
Sheffield Shield Matches	62	96	15	452*	8926	110.19	36
Shield Matches for N.S.W.	31	52	9	452*	4633	107.74	17
Shield Matches for S.A.	31	44	6	357	4293	112.97	19
All Matches for N.S.W.	41	69	10	452*	5813	98.52	21
All Matches for S.A.	44	63	8	369	5753	104.60	25
v. Touring Teams	54	84	8	299*	6259	82.35	25
v. M.C.C. Teams	32	55	5	270	3352	67.04	11

* not out

All references to rules of the game have been left as Sir Donald wrote them and have not been updated or altered from the original text.

Likewise, imperial measurements have been retained. For the contemporary reader, it is useful to note that: 1 inch (2.54 cm) = 12 inches; 12 inches (30.48 cm) = 1 foot; 3 feet (91.44 cm) = 1 yard.

Bradman's discussion of new l.b.w. rules on pages 25–26 relate to the alteration made by the M.C.C. in November 1934, which allowed a ball pitched outside off stump to be defined as an l.b.w. if the batsman stopped it in a line between wicket and wicket.

First published by Associated Newpapers, London, in 1935
Revised edition published by Rigby Limited in 1963.
Reprinted in 2011 by New Holland Publishers (Australia) Pty Ltd
Sydney • Auckland • London • Cape Town

1/66 Gibbes Street Chatswood NSW 2067 Australia
218 Lake Road Northcote Auckland New Zealand
86 Edgware Road London W2 2EA United Kingdom
80 McKenzie Street Cape Town 8001 South Africa

Copyright © 2011 New Holland Publishers (Australia) Pty Ltd

All rights reserved. No part of this publication may be reproduced, stored in a retrieval system or transmitted, in any form or by any means, electronic, mechanical, photocopying, recording or otherwise, without the prior written permission of the publishers and copyright holders.

National Library of Australia Cataloguing-in-Publication entry

Bradman, Donald, Sir, 1908-2001

Don Bradman : how to play cricket / Sir Donald Bradman.

9781742571508 (hbk.)

Cricket--Handbooks, manuals, etc.

796.358
Cover Design: Emma Gough from the Rigby edition
Production Manager: Olga Dementiev
Printer: Toppan Leefung Printing (China) Ltd

10 9 8 7 6 5 4 3 2 1